Catering and Convention Service Survival Guide in Hotels and Casinos

Catering and Convention Service Survival Guide in Hotels and Casinos

Lisa Lynn Backus, CMP, CPCE
and
Patti J. Shock, CPCE, CHT

BEP BUSINESS EXPERT PRESS

Catering and Convention Service Survival Guide in Hotels and Casinos

First published in 2017 by
Business Expert Press, LLC
222 East 46th Street, New York, NY 10017
www.businessexpertpress.com

ISBN-13: 978-1-63157-591-4 (paperback)
ISBN-13: 978-1-63157-592-1 (e-book)

Business Expert Press Tourism and Hospitality Management Collection

Collection ISSN: 2375-9623 (print)
Collection ISSN: 2375-9631 (electronic)

Cover and interior design by Exeter Premedia Services Private Ltd., Chennai, India

First edition: 2017

10 9 8 7 6 5 4 3 2 1

Printed in the United States of America.

Abstract

The job of the Catering Convention Services Manager (CCSM) is varied and diverse. The success or failure of an event can depend on the ability of the CCSM to juggle the components without dropping the ball. Chapters of this book scratch below the surface and impart authors' in-depth industry knowledge that will lead readers from the truth of what a CCSM does on a daily basis versus what the job description states, what emotional and technical skills are required, what employers look for in hiring CCSMs, how to relate to external and internal planners, and execution of catering and convention contracts. It gives an overview of job positions within hotels and facilities that CCSMs will work with necessary to fulfill the contracted legal requirements, providing thorough communication, detailed food and beverage industry information, banquet service styles, menu planning, trade statistics, BEO standards, how to deliver service expectations, and reveals a variety of indoor and outdoor event space setup standards. Included are suggested best practices of working with nonprofits, social, wedding, association, corporate, VIP, celebrity events, and tradeshows. Most chapters will have website links for more information on specific topics and explanations on how this industry operates within casino properties. The final chapters discuss revenue upsell opportunities for *all stakeholders* and industry accounting and the paperwork that pulls this fast-paced catering for convention service business all together.

Keywords

awards, banquets, casino events, catering, ceremonies, conventions, convention services, decor, dinner, entertainment, events, food, meetings, menus, receptions, service

Contents

Foreword

It is an honor and privilege to introduce this book and its authors, Lisa Lynn Backus and Patti Shock. Based on my 40+ years' experience in catering and event planning, I am convinced their collaboration is a beam of clarity to guide as you navigate through the twists and turns of our fascinating profession!

As with every other industry, the hospitality, event, and catering segments are changing rapidly and, unless we keep up or, better yet, stay ahead of the curve, we will not survive in the present competitive marketplace. Event professionals must use every tool available to stay current or be left behind!

It is a win for the catering or event industry when Patti Shock decides to share her vast practical and academic knowledge with an eagerly awaiting audience. Having met Patti in the early 1980s and witnessed her growing contributions to our industry affirms my belief that Patti is truly qualified to write this book. I met and was fortunate to have Patti's advice when I was the national president of the National Association for Catering and Events (NACE). Patti was instrumental in securing the NACE admission to the Convention Industry Council (CIC) and was also the first to receive a grant for the University of Nevada, Las Vegas (UNLV) given by the Foundation of NACE. Her previous books about catering are benchmarks.

This time around, Patti went a step further and collaborated with an industry veteran who brings a proven track record of producing breathtaking and trend setting special events. Lisa Lynn has decades of successfully creating events in numerous environments, each requiring a nuanced set of solutions or needs of adaptation to make the event shine! I worked with Lisa Lynn early in her career and I am thrilled to see her rise to this level of excellence and leadership.

The authors addressed numerous aspects of event planning and covered every step necessary from inception of an idea to the completion of the project. This is also one of the few books to cover every possible locale, indoors or outdoors, permanent or temporary structure, intimate restaurant or immense ballroom, even including the unique world of casinos, notorious for their short-term decision-making process while insisting on spectacular, unique, and absolutely flawless events.

Needless to say, food and beverage is one of the most important ingredients of a successful event. No matter the occasion, joyful or sad, political or social, private or corporate, thousands of years of history confirm, nothing of importance happened in the past, nor will happen in the future, without the host offering the best foods and beverages that are affordable and available.

It is our good fortune to have Patti and Lisa Lynn taking on the task and responsibility to help us advance our knowledge.

Respectfully,

Peter E Gunther, CMP, CPCE
Director, Global Communication, Maxwell Events, Inc.
Director of Catering and Event Planning, Marriott, Retired
President Emeritus of NACE, Founder and President Emeritus of the NACE Foundation

Acknowledgments

The authors have been fortunate enough to have many mentors, colleagues, and friends that have made a difference in their careers.

We don't accomplish anything in this world alone ... and whatever happens is the result of the whole tapestry of one's life and all the weavings of individual threads from one to another that creates something.

—Sandra Day O'Connor

Lisa Lynn would like to acknowledge those who have paved her career path for success for which she gives gratitude to: LaRose Nicholson; Peter Gunther, CMP, CPCE; Rich Benninger; Michele Polci, CPCE, CMP; and her loving and tremendously patient husband Dick Backus, TMW (*the most wonderful*).

Patti would like to acknowledge: John Stefanelli, PhD; Shelley Pedersen, CPCE; William E. Kent, PhD; Timothy M. Lam, MIBS, CHT, CGSP; Marcus M. Lam, CHT, CGSP; and Donnell Bayot, PhD, CPCE, CHE, CFBE.

CHAPTER 1

Introduction to the Catering and Convention Service Field: Your Job Is So Glamorous You Party Every Day

"Your job is so glamorous, you plan parties all day!" Catering and convention service managers (CCSMs) and event planners of all types hear this frequently from others who are in awe of what we do.

The truth behind this infamous curtain of sensationalized perception is that the majority of the time of a CCSM's work is in a standard office environment, or out on the convention floor and juggling a variety of duties.

CCSMs spend good deal of time gathering planner and group information via e-mails, conference calls, and in-person preplanning meetings. They ask a variety of questions to learn about the various groups, their profiles, and guest demographics. Additionally, they seek to understand the meeting planner's objectives and how they prefer their reports to be submitted. All of these are happening while the planners are on a site inspection and fact-finding mission of their own regarding the property, the policies, and the interworking of various departments.

CCSMs struggle with the dynamics of what a planner wants, what their superiors' desire, and how they plan for their guests based on what the actual guest expectation is when their events occur. A good article is *"20 Things Event Planners Say."*[1]

---

[1] www.eventmanagerblog.com/20-things-event-planners-say

For example, a planner may schedule a morning coffee before a meeting when a guest is actually expecting a breakfast. A planner may be on a strict budget and doesn't provide enough coffee for the entire group. This leaves guests unhappy and often believing the hotel did not prepare adequately for them. This is a tough position to be in as a CCSM as you must be professional enough to respond to the guests and not point fingers or blame your planner, and at the same time offer the guest an alternative for purchasing breakfast items within the hotel and inform them of the next time when hosted coffee will be available.

The bulk of time for CCSMs is spent preparing banquet event orders (BEOs) for each event that must be produced by the hotel. For social events such as weddings or galas, there could be 2 to 6 BEOs; for small meetings there could be 10 to 20 BEOs; for really large conventions there can be a few hundred BEOs. Depending on the complexity of the event, it could take 15 minutes to over an hour to create a single BEO.

A typical day for a CCSM without a group in-house could start off with reviewing and prioritizing a list of to-do items made from the previous day, checking e-mails, returning calls, attending file assignment and staff meetings, diving into BEO completions, being interrupted by planner calls for events a year or two from now (*requiring you to open a different file on your desk and opening new screens on your computer*). Sometimes this is followed by the exact same request from another planner, now creating a mess of open files on your desk and computer. Then a sales manager might call to say a planner is coming for an unplanned site visit tomorrow at which time, of course, you already have a preplanning visit scheduled with another group. Your next call is from another sales manager requesting a floor plan diagram for 1,000 guests, classroom style in a ballroom where little other setup information is provided and they won't sign a contract till they see their meeting on a diagram today.

If the day consists of having a group in-house, then we might be to work by 6:30 a.m. for a 7:00 a.m. breakfast followed by the 8:00 a.m. general session, the 10:00 a.m. coffee break, a 12:00 p.m. lunch, 3:00 p.m. coffee break, a reset of the general session room and breakout rooms, the exhibit hall opening, and finding time to fit in more juggling of all of the above. Finally, a 6:00 p.m. reception with a 7:00 p.m. gala event with amazing food, signature drinks, and celebrity entertainment, allowing you to post photos on Facebook and receiving the following feedback from your friends: "*Your job is so glamorous, you plan parties all day!*"

The principal function of a CCSM is to execute a sales contract in all its glory while ensuring planner satisfaction, making money for all stakeholders and, of course, within the planner's budget. Now that is a super successful CCSM!

Catering and Convention Services Manager

This person services meetings, conventions, and social events that are turned over to them from the convention sales or catering sales team.

Catering Sales Manager

Catering sales manager (CSM) makes the initial contact with social or meeting planners without guestrooms. They negotiate and implement the sales contract, which is turned over to the executive director and directors of catering and convention services, who turns them over to the appropriate CCSM after both parties have signed the contract.

Assistant or Associate Director, Director, Executive Director of Catering and Convention Service

These leaders oversee the department and are responsible for the day-to-day operations. Part of their responsibility is to facilitate file assignments from the sales team to a CCSM. Additionally, these positions also perform the tasks of CCSMs.

Hotel Convention Sales Manager

This person is the initial contact with various convention meeting planners, third-party meeting planners and corporate meeting planners. They also negotiate and implement convention sales contracts, which are turned over to the executive director and directors of catering and convention services who in then turns them over to the appropriate CCSM after both parties have signed the contract.

Other titles at some properties include the staffs that perform both the sales and services for groups. These include but are not limited to executive meeting manger, event manager, event coordinator and include in their titles, associate, senior, assistant, or associate director, director and executive director.

A CCSM's duties are all encompassing. They are information central from the planner to other hotel departments on communicating what a catering and convention group will be doing during their time within the hotel.

The duties of a CCSM can consist of any or all of the following:

- Assist sales managers on site visits, creates diagrams prior to contract signing.
- Conduct preplanning meeting and menu tasting after file turn over and before the actual program begins.
- Provide information to hotel departments via an electronically generated document they create called a *group resume*. The resume will have the BEOs, group guest room block pick-up, key contacts, VIPs, arrivals, accounting codes, schedule of events within the conference center, hosted meals, free time, and off-property events. This allows all other departments to staff accordingly for check-in, check-out, restaurant and outlets, valet, housekeeping, exhibit load-in and load-out, and so on.
- Schedule and conduct pre-cons (*pre-convention meetings*).
- Organize planner offering such as banner hanging, person-alized hotel key cards, bell stand room deliveries, marketing and advertising opportunities to planner and their vendors or sponsors.
- Work with the exhibit, decorator, or drayage companies for those groups that have exhibit halls included in their pro-grams (*Often this includes the purchase of hotel items such as ice, cups, electrical, Wi-Fi, etc.*).
- Work directly with planner affiliates on sponsored food and beverage events.
- Prepare floor plan diagrams and fire marshal permit diagrams.

- Coordinate contracted concessions such as amenities and discounts.
- Prepare BEOs and send to planner for approval prior to group arrival and for distribution within the hotel for operations teams.
- React professionally and quickly to pop-up events and unknown onsite changes.
- Arrange planner limos for arrivals and departures.
- Provide daily banquet checks for planner signature approval while group is in-house.
- Advise planner on food and beverage current expenditures compared to the contracted minimum.
- Administer hotel planner recognition program.
- Seek planner participation in the meeting planner satisfaction survey.
- Work with hotel auditing and accounting departments, as well as preferred vendors on final billing.

A career in catering and convention services is an amazing opportunity for the person who is very detailed in their communication proficiencies and who likes a bit of autonomy. The CCSM must have the energy to work long hours and weekends, not be afraid of the unknown and like to coordinate several small items to make one harmonious event. The CCSM must also enjoy being surrounded by controlled commotion, all with proven upsell talents and immense customer satisfaction skills.

The Planners

Meeting planners may have a variety of objectives depending on what type of event, meeting, or convention they are planning.

For the most part, meeting planners come in the following categories:

- Corporate
- Association
- Union
- Nonprofit

- Third-party and independent
- Wedding and social
- Government
- Sports
- Special events

For corporate planners, objectives may be focused around accommodating the demands of their VIPs. Also a *hot-button* for the corporate world is providing exceptional service at every touch point in service. Often the planners take this personally if they believe guests will blame them for something or if the hotel's misgivings are making them look bad to their guests and superiors.

Planners, for expediency, often tend to address the CCSM directly about issues with the hotel that might not meet their expectations such as long lines at the front desk, long lines at the bars or the amount of time it takes their guests to get through catered buffet lines. As if you, the CCSM, can fix each guest's interaction with a multitude of questions for the front desk agent, help them decide what to order from the bar or how they scrutinize the food items on the buffet!

Association and union planners are typically looking for a *wow* at their events. This can include energizing general sessions with entertainment, often with musical introductions. Also, these groups enjoy the latest and greatest in technology: items such as the *catch box*[2] which is a microphone in a tossable box enclosure versus using standard standing audience microphones. Member retention and new member recruitment are top priority to their existence, and conferences with the *wow factor* can be their best tools for engaging members.

The nonprofit planner may focus on reaching the bare minimum in contracted food and beverage guarantees. Additionally, they often rely on monetary sponsorships of their events. Planners have a way to thank these sponsors such as listing their level of contribution on direction or content signage, shout-outs at general sessions, advertisements in printing programs, and so on. In other words, nonprofit events are required to create awareness and raise funds with minimal expenditures. Also the nonprofit

---

[2] Catch Box: https://www.youtube.com/watch?v=apjN3xThfY8 and http://us .getcatchbox.com/pages/_product-overview.

planners depend on receiving tangible donations such as auction items that will generate revenue to fund the meeting, event, convention, future projects, and campaigns. It's important to keep a balance of providing a nonprofit planner with great service while also creating profits for you, your employer, and all stakeholders!

Third-party planners and independent planners are a CCSMs *"frenemy."*[3] These planners are loved for their organization skills, detailed communication tools, and overall knowledge of the industry and the *end user* planner. They can also be a nemesis, known for micromanaging a CCSM and often many other hotel positions.

While a CCSM will show up 15 to 20 minutes prior to a food function, these meeting planners may have been there for half an hour, ordering staff around with changes and additions. CCSMs can learn valuable skills from these planners. They work with CCSMs, hotels, conventions centers, and various planners all around the world, using the best practices from all these experiences onsite at your facilities; don't miss the opportunity to pick up some of their *tricks-of-the-trade*, like conducting a quick operations meeting with key players of the hotel and their staff daily. These meetings are typically held each day of the program to discuss what worked well and areas for improvement that day and more importantly to review the following day's details in the areas of timing, setup room turns, audio-visual specifics and changes, VIP needs, food and beverage pop-ups and cancellations, and so on.

Government meeting planners have a tough job, as it relates to regulations of their industry, per diems, diplomacy, and protocols unique to the government. Additionally, they can be up against hotels or facilities that are limited to working within their budgets and the amount of guestrooms offered to the government rate.

Meeting planners[4] work under different organizational structures. They may work under directors, vice presidents, presidents, any "C" level officer, board(s) of directors, or independently and directly with the planner. The CCSM may have to work with all of the above.

---

[3] Friendly Enemy.
[4] Meeting planner analysis: www.linkedin.com/pulse/20140714172749-4260 8718-the-9-different-types-of-meeting-planners

CHAPTER 2

Required Skill Sets: Apologies, Empathy, and Education

"I'm sorry."
"I apologize."
"Please forgive us."
"Pardon the inconvenience."
"Please accept my apology."
"Please bear with us."
"100 percent my fault."
"I take full responsibility."

For the seasoned CCSM, these can become daily mantras, and no wonder. Planners often express their stress and disappointments directly at the CCSM.

Possible issues which could affect a planner's mood, but which are out of your control, could include:

- Guests complaining about long lines at hotel check-in
- C-level[1] executives whining about not having the best suite in the hotel
- Missing or stolen items from a meeting room
- The attitude of a hotel employee
- The cleanliness of a heavily used restroom
- Issues when guests check-in with a debit card versus a credit card

---

[1] C-level: Chief Executive Officer (CEO), Chief Operating Officer (COO), etc.

- The condition of a guest room or a nonrenovated room or hotel tower
- Lack of hot water or low water pressure in a high-rise hotel
- Hotel running out of nonsmoking rooms when a guest specifically requested nonsmoking
- Guests being checked into rooms that are already occupied
- Fire alarm going off during general sessions and breakouts
- Hotel charges that perhaps a meeting planner didn't prepare for or hasn't paid for in the past, such as:
  o Early check-in fee
  o Wi-Fi charges
  o Resort fees
  o Water station setup costs
  o Charges for re-keying of meeting room
  o Parking fees

Issues unique to Las Vegas:

- A planner fears they will lose guests to the casino
- Perception that morning sessions must start later due to it being a 24-hour party town
- The bell staff not responding in a timely manner to pick up items in the meeting space as they are focusing on hotel check-outs
- Water programs such as pitchers of ice water for classroom setting or events of 20+ guests. Water conservation programs in Las Vegas hotels are in the forefront. Additionally, water is expensive and increasing focus has been made to pass along the charge and add to the revenue stream. Meeting planners may notice fees associated with water that perhaps were not charged for previously. The charges can include: water station charges, pitchers of ice water for meetings, and water not automatically set on at dining tables, but rather provided at a guest's request

The seasoned CCSM can learn and continue to learn in the above environments, skills that can help reduce the stressor affects, sticker shock, and ease a planner's disappointment.

can cause breakage and open a flood of water while damaging the dress, bedding, and carpets. The experienced professional need not to embarrass the guests pointing out the mistake, but rather offer assistance in dry cleaning, moving the room, and possible charges for damage.

A hotel check-in process of using debit cards should be addressed with planners early in the processes. Debit cards are often charged for the daily amount for room, tax and estimated incidental charge holds. This creates a reduction of the amount that a planner can withdraw from an ATM machine, which can be over the amount normally available, leaving the guest without available cash. A well-versed CCSM can accompany the guest experiencing these challenges to the front desk where the front desk agent and the guest call the bank to resolve this and release funds for the guest to access cash via an ATM. Note this must occur during the bank's business days and hours of operation in their particular time zone.

In early preplanning and periodic follow-up conversations on most of these topics, especially those that the planner is not used to paying or didn't plan for, you will need to confirm your planner is knowledgeable on the hotel's processes. Additionally, all of the important items that the planner has relayed to you should be noted in the group resume.[2] Having a *cheat sheet* or company-authorized statement is helpful when your planner asks you to explain why the hotel is charging for items such as:

- Early check-in fees when a room is ready, what they get with the resort fee (*this process is currently being reviewed at the Federal level*).
- Hotels or facilities are now charging for items they pay hard costs for, such as 5-gallon water bottles that are used in water stations and the labor associated to set, fill, and refill these. Also associated with water conservation, especially in areas subject to water drought, are policies on tap water usage such as pitchers of ice water used for meeting room sets.
- Wi-Fi can be controversial, as it is almost expected by the general public to be available and free like many well-known

---

[2] Group Resume: a packet containing all information on a group, including BEOs, Room Setup instructions, schedules, etc.

coffee establishments and not always understood what a large facility actually pays for this service. Wi-Fi can be negotiated separately for public space, meeting space, and sleeping rooms.

- There are multiple processes for offering keys to a planner for their meeting rooms. Keys can range from hard metal to magnetic or digitally coded cards, or door key pads with personalized codes made to duplicate master keys, or a room can be re-keyed and only the key holders have access. This is done for the convenience of the planner to open and unlock their meeting rooms whenever they wish. This should never be considered a means of securing the rooms as an antitheft precaution. Planners should be told that valuables such as laptops, projectors, and personal items such as wallets and purses should not be left in unattended meeting rooms and that if they do so it is at their own risk.

Lastly, there are certain objections planners have sometimes, just perceived fears or prior experience that Las Vegas and other casino cities and facilities face. Most of these are based on a planner's apprehension that guests will not show up for classes, tradeshows, and general sessions based on possible distractions such as gambling, nightlife, and destination-activity offerings. The veteran CCSM will be able to ease the mind of planners and planners by reminding them these offerings will likely attract more guests to register for their conference than that onsite no-show percentage.

Additionally, the skillful CCSM will work with planners to offer and suggest they publicize offerings such as complimentary coffee inside the general session, and exhibitors providing breakfast, lunch and reception food, and beverage inside of exhibit halls.

Education and Training for the Position

Education, training, and a great resume will prepare you for working in catering and convention services. Employers in this field are looking for a combination of education and experience. Often, solid experience will weigh heavier than education for positions that require someone to *hit-the-ground-running*.

Depending on the experience level of the applicant (*entry level, rooms only, small or large group, corporate, social, convention, and the number of rooms or food and beverage minimum*), employers may look for a minimum of a year and a half to five years in a position of catering convention services with a history of hotel or facility experience from positions such as: administrative assistant, banquets, convention setup, culinary, hotel administration and operations, catering and restaurant sales, wedding and event coordination, and so on.

Resume

Your resume is a document that needs to say, "*I am the one for job!*" The purpose of a resume in the catering convention services application process is to get the hiring manager to call you for an interview. The first call is to check the mutual level of interest, how you interact on the phone from the first moment of contact to the closing of the call. On the first or second call you can expect to be offered an in-person interview or an online video and voice interview with Skype or Zoom applications. If on the first call you did not *wow* the employer and jump to the top of the list, you may be told your resume will be kept on file.

During the interview you must be able to show your professionalism and at the same time be humble. Additionally, highlight your experience to match what the posted job description states, such as working with third-party planners (*mention them by company name and program details*). Also, reveal your desire to learn new skills mentioned in the job description such as working with celebrity events and riders. It is acceptable to show your vulnerabilities so future employers can assess if you will be a good fit for the existing team, such as worked conventions up to 200 rooms and looking forward to being part of a team that services groups up to 2,000 rooms. Employers are truly looking for your behaviors at work.

Behaviors revealed during interviews:

- Do you work well as part of a team?
- Do you love this type of work?
- Are you mature enough not to get caught up in work gossip and office politics?

- Do you maintain a positive attitude at all times?
- Are you the type of person that will bring drama to the work environment?
- Is constructive criticism well received?
- Are you worth investing in with training and mentoring?
- Can you handle planner complaints regardless of their professional validity without retaliation?
- Did you dress appropriately for the position at the interview?
- Did you bring copies of your resume to the interview?
- Do you exude confidence?
- How did you prepare and research our company and facility for the interview?
- How do you handle stress?
- Will our planners enjoy working with you?

Employment History

Include work history in order of present-to-past. Under each position held, list briefly duties that show you are experienced in the field such as: handled convention groups of up to 200 rooms on peak, designed wedding packages, specialized in pharmaceutical meetings, exceeded quarterly goals, managed groups with over $500,000 food and beverage minimums, supervised and trained new managers, and so on. If you are new out of college, list intern or externships, volunteer positions and community involvement in lieu of the above in the same format.

Social Media

Employers now routinely check applicant's social media sites, including Facebook, Twitter, Instagram, and so on. Remember that anything you post on social media sites is available for anyone to view. So, be careful what you post.

Memberships and Activities

Networking is a notable part of self-training. Joining professional organizations, whether paid for by an employer or yourself, shows responsibility for taking action to invest in your future rather than be limited to being taught on the job. Joining and attending networking meetings is a start to gaining industry knowledge. Getting involved by volunteering your time on an organization's committee or board of directors allows you to gain experience that sets you apart from most other applicants. This experience allows you to learn and become proficient in fundamental skills like:

- Public speaking
- Planning events for the event industry
- Negotiating on the other side of catering contracts
- Attending national conferences
- Learning Robert's Rules of Order
- Managing financial matters of a local chapter of a national nonprofit organization

Include all your industry association memberships[3] current and past, and your level of involvement. Include networking opportunities, both with local and national chapters that you participate in.

Awards and Recognitions

List all awards, recognitions, or honors you have received to show you have been and will in the future be aggressive with goals, provide exceptional customer service skills, and work within the community. List these dates in order starting with the most recent.

---

[3] • National Association for Catering and Events (NACE) www.nace.net
- Event Service Professionals Association (ESPA) www.espaonline.org
- Hotel Sales and Marketing Association International (HSMAI) www.hsmai.org
- Meeting Professionals International (MPI) www.mpiweb.org
- International Association of Exhibitions and Events (IAEE) www.iaee.com
- International Live Events Association (ILEA) www.ileahub.com
- International CCSMs Association (ICA) www.internationalcaterers.org
- Professional Convention Management Association (PCMA) www.pcma.org

Work Objectives

Note that it's not all that important to list work objectives in a resume, but vital to be ready to confirm them in the interview.

Education

List degrees, diplomas, certificates, certifications, schools attended, industry courses, conference certifications, and on-the-job training required such as: sustainability certified, Forbes training, annual sales training, and so on. List these in date order starting with the most recent.

There are many colleges, junior colleges, and schools that offer degrees and certification in various studies of hospitality management. Among these are:

- California State Polytechnic University at Pomona (Cal Poly) www.calpoly.edu
- Cornell University (CU) www.cornell.edu
- Eastern Carolina University (ECU) www.ecu.edu
- Florida International University (FIU) www.fiu.edu
- Georgia State University (GSU) www.gsu.edu
- Kennesaw State University (KSU) www.kennesaw.edu
- Metropolitan State University of Denver (MSU) www.msudenver.edu
- Michigan State University (MSU) www.msu.edu/
- New Mexico State University (NMSU) www.nsmu.edu
- Northern Arizona University (NAU) www.nau.edu
- Northern Virginia Community College (NVCC) www.nvcc.edu
- Purdue University (PU) www.purdue.edu
- Richland College (RC) www.richlandcollege.edu
- San Jose State University (SJSU) www.sjsu.edu
- The International School of Hospitality (TISOH) www.tisoh.edu
- Virginia Polytechnic Institute and State University (Virginia Tech) www.vt.edu
- University of Houston (UH) www.uh.edu
- University of Central Florida (UCF) www.ucf.edu
- University of Nevada, Las Vegas (UNLV) www.unlv.edu
- University of Southern Mississippi (USM) www.usm.edu

For additional schools, refer to the Council on Hotel, Restaurant and International Education (CHRIE) www.chrie.org.

Certifications

Holding professional certifications show that you have been affording yourself additional on-the-job training and education to advance your career and value in the industry workforce. Some of the most common certifications in catering convention services, meeting planning, and events are:

- CMP—Certified Meeting Professional (from Convention Industry Council)
- CPCE—Certified Professional for Catering and Events (from NACE)
- CSEP—Certified Special Events Professional (from ILEA)
- CMM—Certification in Meeting Management (from MPI)

Licenses and Registrations

- *Food Handlers or Health/Serve Safe/Public Food Cards*: required for selling and servicing food events. These types of cards can include registration, health exam or inoculations, educational training followed by testing to pass and regulation renewals.
- *TAM® (Techniques of Alcohol Management) or Alcohol Awareness Cards*: required for selling and servicing events that include alcoholic beverages.
- *Gaming and Nongaming Card*: from local law enforcement for casino properties with gaming and alcohol.

Training

Currently catering and convention service professionals will need to be proficient in standard Microsoft Office products such as Word, Excel, Outlook, and PowerPoint. Additionally, when working in hotels and facilities knowledge of certain industry-related systems is helpful. For example, hotel systems can be used for the initial guest reservation, front desk check-in, room service, bell desk, concierge, and engineering to communicate about guests' accounts, charging activity, calls, amenities, complaints, and requests.

Software Specific to the Industry

There are several types of sales, catering, convention services, and customer relationship management (CRM) software and facility management programs used in the industry, and we often see some companies purchased by their competitors leading to additional needed training and services. The newer systems are web-based while others are still a standalone desktop application that is restricted to the user's particular operating system version. Among the most popular are:

- Delphi by NewMarket by Amadeus https://amadeus-hospitality. com/
- SalesForce www.salesforce.com
- Daylight www.marketcircle.com/daylite/
- CaterEase www.caterease.com
- Caterware www.caterware.com

Additionally, some systems are specific to golf clubs, nightclubs, institutional facilities, off-premise CCSMs, resorts, and restaurants.

Most of us in the industry today have had little formal training on these systems, but rather have been trained by supervisors, peers, or trial-and-error. This type of on-the-job systems training creates proficiency with experience. And making a few mistakes along the way helps one acquire knowledge of what doesn't work and how to fix it.

Most sales, catering, and convention services professionals have probably used a few of these systems in their career. These operating systems function as the primary CRM, a database of customers and their activity.

The sales, catering, accounting, projection, and analytic functions of these CRM systems include:

- Account and contact information
- Sales outreach tracking
- Holding and reserving of hotel event space (*on prospect, tentative, and definite basis*)
- Merging of contracts and banquet or meeting event documents to documents such as Word, Excel, and PDFs
- Creating and revising BEOs and their corresponding checks
- Banquet reconciliation of consumption, posting of revenue, and check closing
- Auditing and accounting of the group
- Financial forecasting of revenue
- Operational tool for staffing and food ordering and production
- Analytical data extraction for reporting customer booking and buying trends, precedent setting and repetitious behavior

These are used in conjunction with software and point-of-sale (POS) systems that record revenue with internal hotel systems such as MICROS, OPERA, and InfoGenesis, just to name a few.

Among the more popular software programs for creating room-set diagrams are:

- Meeting Matrix: www.meetingmatrix.com
- Delphi Diagrams: http://delphi-diagrams.software.informer.com/
- Social Tables: www.socialtables.com
- AllSeated: www.allseated.com (free)
- Room Viewer; www.roomviewer.com

Some of these systems are available online for the meeting planners and the public in general to draw their own diagrams.

CCSMs will need to become experts at their property in creating many different kinds of room sets. Unfortunately, hotel specifications listed in marketing materials and online information is not always correct. These list the maximum set without anything else in the room. It's quite rare that a room would not have anything other than a maximum set of tables and chairs.

Room sets often include combinations of the following:

- *Staging*: of various sizes, head tables on stages, podiums, lecterns, flags, and so on.
- *Audio-visual* (AV): including microphones, front-screen projection, rear-screen projection, overhead "flying" of screens, technician tables, camera risers, and so on.
- *Water stations.*
- *Banquet equipment*: such as food and beverage buffets, tray jacks, and so on.
- *Planner signage and materials.*

As you become more seasoned as a CCSM, including developing competency within your company culture, you will learn additional skills that will provide you with knowledge of how to handle complex planner responses and preparing yourself for future promotions.

Some of these responses will be suggestions on room setup for guest safety, communicating (*but not libeling yourself or employer*) on local laws such as smoking, emergency preparedness, how you will manage events during construction, theft and criminal activity, under-age drinking, and gaming regulations.

You will begin to focus more on your career goals knowing when to identify occasions to *manage up*, a term for communicating to senior leadership, thereby letting them know about your bigger picture ideas, tasks you can take off their plate and overall keeping them in the loop on items that could keep them out of trouble. Of course it's wise to know their favorite current event topics and to always be there to provide them their favorite beverage or seat at events.

Finally, look for opportunities to take on projects that will provide experience in project management, training, and supervisions of others. Create a personal brand for yourself that is memorable, sophisticated, moving forward with company initiatives and—above all—a positive *can do* attitude that is drama-free.

CHAPTER 3

What Planners Really Want: Relationships

Whatever side of the industry you are a part of, it is critically important to develop rapport and to understand the goals, needs, and desires of the planner, sponsor, the hotel, and the media.

Planner and CCSM Relationships

Starting with the initial sales process, a planner can be wary of what and how much the hotel will be charging for in sleeping room rates, resort fees, taxes, and meeting space rental. After the contract is signed planners may find a sense a relief and are ready to start the planning with the CCSM. During this time when a CCSM should be focusing on relationship building in the planning process, other obstacles can present themselves. Often the planner will find that there are other fees associated with conducting meetings and events within the contracted meeting space. Most of the fees are covered in a small clause in the contract that states something like "*current catering policies apply*."

It is the responsibility of the CCSM to communicate to the planner what additional fees they are responsible for in a manner that explains their purpose, with that message being delivered both confidently and eloquently. Such conversations can evoke emotional responses from the planner such as disappointment, anger, and hurt—responses like "*I have never paid for water stations before*" or "*this hotel is too difficult to work with; I am never returning*." This is mostly attributed to the inexperience of the planner, lack of budgeting for operational fees, and an overall feeling in the back of their minds that hotels are trying to sell them something at all times.

Getting past obstacles will be essential in the relationship building with planners. The CCSM must earn their planner's respect. Respect comes from when the planner can see you know your job, including when you don't have the answer to all their questions that you DO know how and who to get answers from quickly. Additionally, planners will appreciate that you have anticipated their needs by knowing their program inside and out. The planner will look to you as the expert in your property, company, and city. Planners will, in due course, trust you enough to lean on you for advice in making suggestions and recommendations that are frustrating or causing inertia to them. A CCSM can make statements like "*I can see this is difficult for you, so here is how I can help you,*" and explain what you can and will do. Or "*I am here to help you through this; let me know your most important meeting objective for us to achieve together.*" It is at that point where CCSMs provide clear solutions and options that will remove the planner's frustration that the relationships with the CCSM moves forward as a true partnership and as an extension of the planner's team!

Let's elaborate on an important part of knowing your planner's program "*inside and out.*" Ideally your planner has provided detailed documents months ahead of time that includes for each meeting room and each date the times, room setup specifics, audio-visual and IT requirements, and food and beverage details. Although this is not 100 percent fantasy on the CCSM's part, it can happen every once in a while. When this doesn't happen, a CCSM must find out piecemeal all the details so they can understand the entire program. The ideal time for this is during onsite preplanning meetings and conference calls. If a planner is not getting you the details you need, suggest a monthly (*and eventually weekly*) conference call to address specifics. A CCSM is wise to focus on one topic at a time. An example would be a call on reviewing meeting room assignments, their scheduled event times, possible room set turns (*meaning the room might be set for theater and then turn for the next meeting to crescent rounds*). The next call could be on learning the food and beverage plan events. In all of these calls, the CCSM will need to drill down by asking specific questions with an attention to details on operations from the hotel side, while planners gain service level expectations. For example, a planner may tell you that all meals will be served in their exhibit hall. The questions to ask are:

- What menus have you planned?
- Where will the guests be coming from prior to the meal?
- Where will they go after the meal?
- Is seating provided for meals or are guests expected to roam the tradeshow floors while eating?

With answers to these questions, the CCSM will be able to explain the operational side to the planner with suggestions. For instance, if your property has a standard for paper and plastic products only (*no china, glass, or silverware*) for tradeshows, this can be communicated to the planner by explaining that it allows the guests to eat standing and to visit tradeshow booths, then disposing of service items in trash receptacles placed along the tradeshow floor. This allows more time for guests to spend directly with exhibitors at their booths. Exhibitors, in turn, benefit by having more attention focused on them rather the meal being held in a function room without exhibitor interaction.

Lastly, there are still *old school* relationship builders and maintainers that hold up even in today's busy cyber world. These include taking planners to dinner or other *bread-breaking* meals. This allows you to treat the planner to pleasant activities (*not costing them money*), thereby putting them in an open and grateful mindset. They begin to open up about themselves with personal detailed information such as where they live, marital status, children, pets, free time activities, and food and beverage preferences. Make notes in your CRM systems of planner likes and special nuances for future communications.

Generally, a planner that tells you what they want, what they are not fond of, and reminds you of these items more than once will be a relationship you can manage well. Be cautious of those planners who do not express the wishes and are hard to get to know.

Check in frequently with planners during their events or on the convention floor to see what they need at that particular time and follow up quickly with tasks and solutions. What's important to your planner should be tremendously important to you.

Meeting planners of all types LOVE complimentary industry perks, and who doesn't. Perks such as suite upgrades, welcome and mid-program amenities, limo transfers, show tickets, staff meals, and the ever-popular spa treatments!

Sponsorships are growing, due to the ability to target market segments and because television advertising is not as effective now that viewers can record and fast-forward through commercials.

If you are planning a press conference for the media, provide at least three days' notice. Schedule the event early in the day so the reporter can make the evening news. Friday tends to be a slower news day, so it is the best day to schedule a press conference. Saturday and Sunday are not good days because a smaller news crew is typically scheduled. Let them know if there will be food available, as food is a draw for most reporters.

Relationship Builders

- Smiles
- Make people feel at ease; no one wants to feel ill at ease
- People gravitate to people who make them feel comfortable
- Know when to say please
- Know how to say I'm sorry
- Know how to say thank you
- Know how to give and receive compliments

The customer is not always right

- The **RIGHT** customer is always right
- Not all customers are created equal
- Some buy a lot from you, respect your opinions, and pay their bills on time
- Some just really drain you with small orders, constant complaining, and late payments

Planners Have Choices

- They want to be convinced that booking with you is the right choice.
- In other words, that their event will be done right!

Building a Sense of Community

Two of the most basic of human needs are a sense of belonging and a need for nourishment. Over the centuries, the communal meal or the act of *breaking bread* together has been an important element in maintaining the family and may include friends. No one ever enters an Italian grandmother's house without being offered food and drink.

Here are some suggestions on how to bring that feeling of belonging to your events?

- *Hospitality desk in the lobby*: for guests checking in or in the group registration area. Offer complimentary drinks, snacks, and conversation, where permitted.
- *Family style service*: platters are set on the banquet table for guests to pass around and serve themselves. This option should only be for small groups with three courses or less. (*Be sure the hotel has plenty of lightweight platters. And avoid entrees in heavy sauces, especially red sauces. Splatters happen!*)
- *Tastings*: wine, beer, coffee, tea, cheese, chocolate, game, even apple varieties, and so on.
- *New exotic foods*: introduce foods from other countries to start a conversation, such as reindeer pate[1] or mangosteen.[2]
- Make refreshment breaks interactive. Have guests create their own snacks from ingredients provided, such as plain cupcakes with different icings and toppings. This gets conversation and laughter going as everyone shows off their masterpieces. Also popular are trail mix components.

---

[1] http://foodbeast.com/content/2011/12/01/reindeer-pate/

[2] www.mangosteen.com/

The Catering Convention Services
Sales-to-Service Process

The simplistic sales-to-service process consists of:

- Initial sales call by a sales manager or an RFP (*request for proposal*) sent by the planner or meeting planner
- Proposed list of room availability, services, and pricing
- Site inspection and selection visit
- Contracting for the agreed event, convention, or tradeshow
- Turnover of contract to the servicing teams
- Execution of events, including postevent accounting
- Thank you and welcome back for future programs

For standard hotel and conventions centers, the process begins with the sales process.

The most common ways this is initiated:

- Planner or meeting planner calls directly to hotel sales managers or regional managers that they have developed relationships with during their career.
- Planner or meeting planner develops an RFP[3] and sends out to the hotels sales departments, convention, and visitor bureaus or third-party planners.
- Third-party planner sends out RFPs to hotels sales departments, conventions, and visitor bureaus.

Request for Proposal

An RFP form includes information that a hotel sales manager can review to determine if the business opportunity is an appropriate fit for both parties.

---

[3] Request for Proposal.

The guts of an RFP are what we call in old-school terms *rates, dates, and space* data. The availability of the hotel and its facilities, sleeping room rates, and facility rental on planner's desirable dates will determine its viability.

But not all sales processes include RFPs. They can be as simple as a phone call to the sales manager. Often planners with long-standing relationships with sales managers may want to begin with an informal process.

Contracting

At such time that planner or meeting planners and hotel sales managers have agreed to move forward with a formal sales contract, then additional processes are initiated. Often, the details for the contract are sent to the BR (*business review*) committee meeting where members of the sales team and directors determine if it is viable for the company as a whole. In many organizations an executive approval from director or vice presidents of sales is sufficient for approving legal documents. If the contract is approved, it is then sent to the contract signer who may have not been the meeting planner involved in the negotiation but rather the group's "C" level, vice presidents, owners, or legal teams, among others, for signature approval.

File Turnover

Once the contracts are signed by the group and countersigned by the sales team it is ready to be put through the turnover process to the catering convention services team. After all the gathering of pertinent documents, including the signed or countersigned contract, documented approvals and forms, deposit confirmation and miscellaneous documents, the turnover packet is e-mailed out. Departments or individuals receiving these turnovers can include the directors of catering convention services, group rooms coordinator, audio-visual suppliers, and other key hotel departments.

When the director of catering convention services receives the file turnover they assign one or more CCSMs to the group. The CCSMs will send the planner an e-mail introduction of themselves letter, followed by a follow-up phone call. At this time, they may send additional information to the planner such as guidelines or policies not covered in the contract as well as current catering menus.

Execution of the Contract

At the start of this chapter we mentioned the sales process in its simplistic terms. It is, of course, anything but simplistic. After the contract is signed and turned over to catering and convention services, it is a complex and time-consuming activity to drill down in order to find what all the components of the program are. These can include, but are not limited to:

- Schedule of events for the entire program
- Food and beverage specifications
- Meeting room setup
- Audio-visual requirements
- IT—Internet technology requirements
- Exhibit and trade show arrangements
- Third-party planners or other companies the planner has contracted with
- Reviewing contract concessions
- Potential outside or off-property events
- Resolving any noncontracted issues
- VIP arrangements
- Preplanning site visits
- Overall planner expectations for all of the above

The drill-down process can be ongoing throughout the planning process, and you can expect the unexpected for program additions, changes, and even changes to the additions.

As the planning formalizes and the program nears, the CCSM is diligently preparing for the group arrival. The main forms of communication to hotel operations teams are BEOs (*banquet event orders*), group resumes, and information shared at the earlier held pre-con meeting. When the group is onsite, the CCSM assists them with meeting requirements and overseeing the operations of registration, room setup, food and beverage. After the group and its planners depart, the CCSM submits final accounting, sends thank you e-mails or letters, and files group folders under completed events.

However, rarely is this the last of working with this group on this particular program. Frequently, the correspondence, issues regarding lost items, their thank-you letters, post-event issues from guest surveys, complaints or billing discrepancies can continue for several weeks.

Gratuities, Tips, and Service Charges

Gratuities: Gratuities are mandatory and are added to the bill. They can range from 18 to 24 percent of the total bill. Gratuities belong to the staff, and the hotel is not allowed to keep any portion of the monies.

Tips: Tips are voluntary, like when you are in a restaurant. If service is exceptional, planners may add a tip on top of the mandatory gratuity, or they may tip specific individuals for services rendered.

Service Charge: Most people would think that the service charge is for service, but hotels can keep a portion of this fee. Many sales people will say that the service fee is non-negotiable, but some meeting planners say they ask what it covers, and have been able to negotiate away part of the fee by eliminating part of the services.

It is important to note that some distribution rules are defined by individual state laws. For example, in Massachusetts gratuities must be distributed in their entirety to frontline service personnel. Also, in some states, taxes may not be charged on top of the gratuity, but added to the total after computation of taxes. In some states the portion of service that is directly paid to servers in gratuity is not taxed while the portion of the service charge that is paid to the "house," meaning hotel, is taxed. For example, if the hotel service charge is 24 percent and the servers get 15 percent of the 24 percent, it is nontaxable. The remaining 9 percent of the 24 percent retained by the "house" is taxable.

In most of the states, service charges are collected by the house and redistributed as the management sees fit. While a good part of the service charge goes to the service staff, often a portion is kept by the house for bonus or commission payment to catering sales or conference services managers, with the remainder going to the overall bottom line of the property. Again, the tax issue tends to be governed by state law, but many states charge tax on top of the service charge.

One of the items most professionals miss with this issue is the effect on server or employee compensation and its subsequent effect on the skill level of banquet or catering service staff.

In part, server compensation at gratuity-based properties seems to require a higher level of record keeping, as the gratuity *pool* for each event must be kept separate and divided by the staff that worked the event. The result is relatively transparent compensation to service staffs and they feel reasonably compensated for their work, resulting in attracting a higher level of professionalism, loyalty, and dedication to service.

With a service charge-based compensation model, the compensation becomes far less transparent. Record keeping is made easier by allowing the property to create a "*tip pool*" for the pay period–the total amount of service charges are divided by the total work hours of service personnel for the pay period, resulting in an hourly wage or "share" (*e.g., $10,000/500 labor hours = $20.00/hour*). The total amount of compensation to an individual is based on the number of hours worked multiplied by the dollar amount of the share. While easier from a record-keeping standpoint, this method is much less transparent to the frontline worker in a variety of ways. In general, the house rarely discloses to the planner how much of the service charge is actually directed to worker compensation and how much is directed to the house.

Examples of how this has played out: At one property, all catering managers and CCSMs were allotted 40 hours in the tip pool per week, adding to the number of labor hours and reducing the frontline hourly wage. While this serves to incentivize the manager, it can discourage professional service personnel, as it reduces their overall compensation. At one property, it did not stop with middle management, but upper-level management (*from assistant director to the higher levels, further diluting the tip pool*).

At another property, the compensation for workers ranged from $14.00 to $18.00 per hour, depending on what the resulting calculations regarding the tip pool were. On the one hand, this meant that servers were always guaranteed to make at least $14.00 per hour. On the other, if the hourly wage calculated out to $20.00 per hour, then all additional monies above the $18.00 per hour were shown as revenue toward the catering or conference services budget. Because the property was located in an area with a small labor pool, the director of the department proposed doing away with the $18.00 ceiling in order to attract and retain a more highly skilled worker. Upper management refused because they did not want to lose the revenue that the additional money from the service charges provided to the bottom line.

This kind of situation results in a lower level of service and a less-professional staff. Why work in this department if one is highly skilled, when one could be better compensated for less work by being a restaurant server, for example?

Fixed and Variable Costs

While people are complaining about the high cost of food at catered events, they are not considering the overhead that a hotel has to cover in the price of the food. Overhead includes both fixed and variable costs. Fixed costs would include the mortgage or lease payments, insurance, investment in furniture, fixtures, and equipment (FFE), salaried positions, and so on. Variable costs would include the cost of food; heating, air conditioning, or ventilation (HVAC); hourly salaries; printing; and so on.

The Cost of That Muffin

One of the largest expenses is labor. Let's look at that muffin on the continental breakfast table. How many people are involved in getting that muffin on the table? Someone has to put it on the menu and have the menu printed. Someone has to take the order and create the BEO. The BEO goes to the chef, who orders the ingredients from the purchasing manager. Someone receives the delivery on the loading docks and gets it put into inventory. The cooks then need to requisition the ingredients from the storeroom and bake the muffin.

Meanwhile, porters are cleaning and vacuuming the meeting room. The banquet setup crew then comes in with the tables and chairs, followed by the banquet service people who requisition the linen from the laundry and the utensils from the storeroom and set up the table. The engineer has to be sure the room is the proper temperature. Then there is a banquet server that keeps the table refreshed during the function.

At the end of the function, the staff needs to come in and break down the room and send the dirty linen to the laundry and everything else (*dishes, utensils, etc.*) back to the stewarding department (*they wash the dishes*) and then to storage.

At casino properties, the cost of a 24-hour operation is staggering. It costs upwards of $1 million per day to just keep the doors open.

If you want cheap muffins, you could always go get them at Costco and feed your guests in a public park. But, in a hotel, you have to pay for the labor, overhead, and the service.

Food doesn't cost that much in comparison to the overall event, photographers can cost just as much as a caterer sometimes. We are in a very labor-intensive business, and we have to deal with perishable foods and waste.

CHAPTER 4

Contracts and Their Execution: The Agreement

A contract is a legally binding agreement between two or more parties. While oral agreements may be enforceable, they are more difficult to prove, so we recommend that ALL contracts be in writing.

A legal contract must contain the following elements:

1. An Offer.
2. Acceptance of the Offer.
3. Consideration for each party (*Consideration can be money, a product, or a service.*).
4. Capacity or Authority. Signers must be competent, of legal age, sound mind, and have legal authority.
5. Time Element (*When must the elements of the contract be met?*).

Convention Services, Catering and Rooms-Only Contracts

Weeks and even months of negotiations by the planner and sales manager can lead up to the sales contract. During this time, sales managers have offered a specified number of guest rooms at a discounted rate and provided the appropriate amount of meeting space for the amount of guest rooms the planner is willing to commit to.

Industry contracts are standardized documents that need to have signature approval from both parties (*the facility and the planner contract signer*) to be legally binding. These contracts set forth conditions of mutual responsibility. For example, the hotel agrees to hold the agreed number of guest rooms over specific dates and the planner agrees to pay the rate and fill these rooms with guests over these same dates. This goes for the other contracted items such as room types and rates, meeting space held, and concessions offered. Like any legal document, contracts include a whole slew of clauses. Below are standard clauses that a CCSM must be familiar with so as to be able to speak knowledgeably with the planner:

- *Room attrition*[1]: This clause informs planners of the mutual commitment of hotel rooms over the contracted dates. It often offers the release of a certain percentage of rooms by a cutoff date (*usually 30 days before the first day of the contracted rooms*). If a planner exercises this clause, their room commitment liability is reduced. Room attrition can be a common issue that CCSMs will face with planners. This can occur for a variety of reasons, such as the planner didn't generate enough interest in their program for guests to register, changes in the economy where employers or guests are not spending as much money on travel and education or conferences, inexperienced planners overestimated the number of guests rooms, guest have loyalties to other hotel brands, guests use travel websites to find better rates, and being at the headquarter hotel is not as important as the per night rate, to name just a few. A CCSM can advise periodically with *pick-up* reports that show where the planner stands on amount of rooms with guests currently holding reservations. Note this can change daily with additions and cancellations.

  Savvy meeting planners have incentive tricks up their sleeves to attract meeting guests, sponsors, and exhibitors to book within the contracted room block. Among these are: lower registration fees and *early bird* discounts, prizes for guests that book within the block, refusing registration to the conference without a room reservation, refusing of shipments to the hotel without a room reservation, and so on.

  Another item the hotel can do is run an *around the block* report that matches up the planner's registration list by name

---

[1] Attrition: see Experient Guide to Room Block Management www.experient-inc.com/solution/publications/gtrbm/guide_rbm_08.pdf

to the hotel's reservations not listed in the block via group reservation code. Guest may have booked a reservation but not been given the group code at the time of reservation. Most hotels choose to do this only if the group room block did not fill, only by request and following the last day of the conference or after the last guest checks out. This process can be tricky in large properties, especially if the name of the guest is different on the convention registration (*such as Robert Smith*) versus the hotel registration (*such as Bob Smith*).

- *Accommodation, rates, and cutoff dates*: These combined clauses show a grid of the dates, number of rooms held, the room category type such as king- or double-bedded rooms, suites, and the popular catch-all ROH (*run-of-house*) rooms. The rates are listed for those specific dates and room categories as well as the last day or cutoff date for guests to book at that rate. After the cutoff date, the rates typically return to the current prevailing selling rate, also known as the *rack rate*. Noted in the contract will be reservation type, such as rooming list (*provided by the planner*) and call-in where guests call in directly or reserve via an online link. A note about ROH rooms—these are typically the lowest price rooms and the rooming coordinator or front desk manager can assign these just about anywhere in the hotel. Some contracts will include rooms-resell and no-lower-rate-offered clauses, and many planners may know this long before you do—especially third-party planners monitoring the hotel rates for planners.

- *Deposits, payment dates, or billing*: These clauses will note the amount of earnest money to be paid to the hotel as the initial deposit and the dates of scheduled deposits. More often than not these deposits are nonrefundable and if not paid as listed will make the contract null and void. The billing clause may list parameters for direct billing for those with credit history and payment in full for those events such as catering-only, social, and international groups. A CCSM should watch this closely and invoice accordingly or alert their billing department for their current expected charges based on food and beverage minimums or actual BEO orders.

- *Force majeure*: This clause allows either party to cancel the contract based on *acts of God* or incidents including natural disasters, war and acts of terrorism, governmental sanction, and other emergencies with no or substantially reduced penalties or liability. When this presents itself to the CCSM, it should be referred to the directors and sales departments to implement.

- *Food and beverage minimums*: This clause provides the minimum a planner must spend for this particular contract. This is traditionally consumable food and beverage provided by the banquet team. Also, this is almost always BEFORE tax and service charges. It is important that a CCSM confirms with planners that they understand exactly what items are applied to the minimum and that tax and service charges are not included. There may be some situations in larger hotels where group events in alternative hotels and onsite restaurant outlets will be included in the overall food and beverage minimum. This applies to hotels and outlets within same ownership where guests are encouraged to patronize and not venture off to competing properties. Groups that do not reach their food and beverage minimums can be charged in a variety of ways, depending on the property. Most often the group is charged the difference of the actual spending and the minimum. Most CCSMs will encourage planners to upgrade their orders in order to get them closer to the minimum expenditure. Some planners become shrewd about this, knowing they will not be charged tax and service charge on this differential.

   It's also important for the CCSM to know what the planner's objective is for sponsors, exhibitors and affiliate food and beverage not covered in the contract but a vital part of their program and revenue expected to be included in the group's overall food and beverage minimum. Ask for a history of how much revenue these groups produced.

- *Cancellation policy*: This clause allows either party to cancel the contract and provides the appropriate method, such as in writing. It also lists the dollar amount of the cancellation fee. This fee may be on a sliding scale related to the number of days prior to the first date of the contracted event. Sometimes it is less expensive for planners to cancel a contract rather than execute it due to various circumstances such as corporate mergers, internal changes in leadership, date changes, legal matters, and so on. Most of the time, in larger hotels, cancellations are handled by the sales team.

- *Concessions*: This is usually the first part of a contract that CCSMs will look at when the group file is turned over to them. This is because it is the most negotiable and customized part of the contract. A CCSM will look this over to see what they are dealing with and what to anticipate with respect to the group. The concession clauses can be quite long depending on the value of the group. Many hotels or facilities will actually list the amount of the concessions, showing to the meeting planner their retail value in hard dollars. Common concessions are one complimentary room per 40 rooms booked, 10 percent discount off of prevailing catering menu pricing, complimentary staff office, Wi-Fi, and VIP welcome amenities. Concessions might also include a specified number of VIP round trip limousine transfers, a specified number of room upgrades to the best available at the reduced group rate, spa discounts, complimentary or discount staff rooms, reduced or eliminated resort fee, discounts on audio visual, discounted shipping, receiving or storage charges, complimentary risers, podiums and easels, and so on. Sometimes the concessions seem to be (*from a CCSM's perspective*) the most difficult to manage, such as restaurant meal vouchers, bottles of water in the room each day, one-and-a-half cups of coffee per person—not ordered by the gallon, construction, and noise. And some concessions can seem *over-the-top*, such as very large rebates to the master account.

- *Other clauses*: There are many standard legal, corporate, and property-specific clauses that may be required by your legal department. Be sure you know how to address these, even if it is to say, "*that can best be addressed by our legal department.*"

Finally, there are times when you can expect the unexpected. These may come in the form of double bookings in which sales managers have double booked the same meeting room over the same dates, where planners have made mistakes and not booked their rooms correctly to match their meeting space dates, where contract verbiage isn't clear enough on the exact meaning of something (*usually in the concessions area*). When these contract issues arise, the best approach is to bring this to the attention of the catering and convention services director(s) and include a possible resolution, and then together bring this to the attention of the sales managers and finally to the planner for resolution. Often the solution will only require change orders or addendums to the contract. In unfortunate situations—and as last resort—it may cause the moving of one or more groups to another facility or cancellation of the entire contract.

Rarely, but it happens, you will be required to address items within your hotel (*because, after all, your planner expects you to know everything*) that are not necessarily a contract issue but a hotel operations issue. Examples of this might be the policy on bed bugs, human trafficking, elevator and escalator repair, perceived lack of hotel labor, lack of free Wi-Fi, and so on.

Some thoughts on Sales 101 as it pertains to executing contracts:

Old Sale Adage #1: "*The sales manager sells the dream and the service manager services the nightmare.*" Not too much has changed with this well-known industry statement over the years, as many a CCSM can relate to (*mostly under their breath or in their mind as they are forced to listen to a planner's rant*).

Old Sales Adage #2: "*Nothing happens if it doesn't get sold first.*" Another key duty of a CCSM is the responsibility to be an extension and back-up for the sales team, providing them information, knowledge, and diagrams as needed to book groups and beat out the competition. If there is something slightly misaligned in the contract after the turnover process, the first route of solution is for the CCSM to find a remedy. These issues can range from a minor mistake in a concession item to a large problem like a double-booked general session room. Solutions can be found by looking at all the space, then determining if other groups or events can be moved around to accommodate all group events. Additionally, having a transparent relationship with planners, to be able to have conversations on subjects of a sensitive nature, is very helpful. Your next step is to seek advice from your leadership with a concise explanation of the problem and your potential solution(s) to the problem. If you don't have a solution, let leadership know what your research has revealed.

Old Sales Adage #3: "Happy planners tell a few friends, unhappy planners tell a few dozen friends." While this is still true, social media has made this instantaneous from a few dozen to a few thousand. We see this occasionally with guests in long lines at check-in suddenly posting on convention blogs and Instagram that there are exaggerated wait times. Chances are, when guests have their heads down and glued to their smartphones, someone is reading about their experience as it is happening. These days, nothing can kill the good momentum between the planner and the hotel quicker than guests posting negative reviews on social media. A CCSM should also be following the planner's apps and Twitter feeds, among others. Be prepared to handle social media issues before the planner brings them to your attention. Work with the front desk to know what the current wait times are, let the planner know the strategy for expediting the wait times, and so on. These types of intangible unwritten duties of a CCSM can faithfully show how you can anticipate the needs of the planner.

Here are some legal terms that CCSMs should be familiar with:

Breach of contract: A legal action when a contract is not honored by one or more of the parties, because of nonperformance or interference with the other party's performance.

Damages: Awards, typically financial, as compensation for loss or violation of contract.

Penalties: Punishments imposed for breaching a contract.

Fraud: Intended deception for financial or personal gain.

Liabilities: Obligations, being responsible for something.

Letter of agreement: A letter of understanding. It can be enforced the same way as a contract if it contains the elements of a contract.

APEX

APEX stands for *Accepted Practices Exchange* and is an initiative of the Convention Industry Council.[2] The purpose is to bring industry professionals together to standardize formats for RFPs, contracts, terminology, and so on.

The APEX contracts best practices guide offers guidance about various aspects of industry contracts to event organizers, hoteliers, and other tourism and hospitality industry professionals.

The APEX contracts materials are not intended to develop an industry *standard* document, but to provide an overview of voluntary accepted practices for negotiations for the use of hotel and event space. These materials should not be construed as a substitute for legal advice. Industry professionals are encouraged to seek legal advice regarding contracts and other legal matters, as no single contract will work perfectly for every event.

Download the APEX contract accepted practices guide here: www.conventionindustry.org/APEX/AdditionalResources.aspx

Negotiation

When you ask colleagues why they are attending a meeting, you usually get answers like, networking, education, etc. But when they return and you ask how the meeting was, they usually start describing the food and beverage events. So food and beverage is important to the success of your meeting.

People generally remember only the very bad or the excellent events they have attended. You don't want to be remembered for bad events (*skimpy food, cheap booze, tacky theme, etc.*), you don't want to be in the middle where the event is promptly forgotten, you want to be remembered for the fabulous events that guests talk about for years.

Catering is usually the largest budget item for most meetings. Yet, it often comes last in the planning process. Planners often call food and beverage events a "*black hole.*" They don't know what is negotiable or how to negotiate. Catering is not one-size-fits-all. Everything about each event is unique.

---

[2] www.conventionindustry.org

Soft Costs Versus Hard Costs

One thing to consider is soft costs versus hard costs. Hard costs are anything the hotel has to put out money for. A hotel cannot sell a bottle of wine for $40.00 if they paid $50.00 for it, but the CCSM can recommend a less expensive wine that is affordable and of good quality. Soft costs can be meeting room rental charges, because the hotel does not have to outlay cash. They can also include the room with the view, limo pickup for VIPs, free or reduced parking, a comp microphone in the room, corkage, and so on.

The most negotiable things to negotiate are contents of a menu. If a planner wants to swap out items, or create a custom menu, that is much easier to get approval from leadership than it is to discount menu prices.

So, what is least negotiable? Minimums. You have to be sure to protect the space you are holding and ensure it will be offset with either a high enough food and beverage purchase or rental fees.

Also difficult to negotiate: Labor fees and service charges. Especially in a unionized property as the collective bargaining agreement drives these fees. There is no way not to pay for them.

Occasionally, a CCSM will receive a group turnover where the contract that is less than desirable to execute. These can include some of the following issues.

- Double booking of meeting space
- Confusing concession items
- The contract signer is not the planner
- Space held on a 24-hour basis without listing what event the space is held for
- Group information, history, and profile not offered in the booking details

Double Booking of Meeting Space

Unfortunately, it happens that a contract gets manipulated to offer space that is already contracted to another group. Generally this happens in the conversion of systems to a word document. The word document can be adjusted to add what is not available in the CRS system.

When this double booking of space is caught it can be an easy or an extremely difficult situation to fix. Sometime this means swapping out a room that a group might not need to a group that does. Regardless of the resolution it is always a difficult conversation to have with at least one of the meeting planners if not both.

The first step to finding contractual errors is for the CCSM to compare the contracted space in the CRS system such as Delphi and compare to the contracted space. If any discrepancies are found then the next steps are to find what other group has booked the space and begin to look for solutions. This is also the perfect time to check that meeting space date aligns with the date of the contracted rooms. Check to be sure that the peak date of the room block has adequate space to accommodate the number of guests the following day.

Solutions can come in many forms from finding alternative spaces to moving events around. Hopefully, solutions are met with agreement with all parties involved and without a group cancelling or moving to another property.

Before speaking with planners it is best to have discussed this with directors and sales manager or directors for their input. Often the directors will reach out to the planners on your behalf. Letting planners know their space contracted is not available to them is never a comfortable conversation to have. More often than not a solution of some sort is implemented but the honesty relationship with the hotel is compromised.

Confusing Concession Items

Concessions are items listed in the contract that are offerings by the hotel as complimentary or at a discount.

Some of the typical offerings are:

- Discounted guestrooms
- Complimentary guestrooms and suites
- Discounted rates offered days pre and post of the contracted dates
- Percentage discounts on food and beverage

- Special menus discounted
- Percentage discounts on audio visual
- Internet discounts
- Early check-in and late check-out
- Discounted resort fees
- Complimentary parking

Concession offerings can be confusing when not written for clarity. Sometimes the concessions can be interpreted differently by the planner, the sales manager, and the CCSM.

For example, the sales contract may offer in writing discounted rates for "guestrooms" three days prior and three days after the contracted dates. However, the planner may want to extend a suite and is denied, as the hotel does not offer date extensions for suites. The planner may not have understood the guestroom and the suite are not the same and was confused by this.

Often an Internet concession will state "complimentary internet in staff office." The interruption can be difficult if there is more than one staff office. Furthermore, it doesn't state how many devices or number of people it will cover in a "staff office." Additionally, it doesn't mention if this Internet is a hard line or Wi-Fi.

Also a planner must review all menus carefully as some items such as package all-day breaks might be not available for discounts as they are already discounted.

Contract Signer Is Not the Planner

Often contracts are signed by company presidents, owners, directors, and so on. However, they are not the main group planner contacts.

CCSM will send an intro letter to whoever is listed as the contact on the contract only to be corrected by the contract signer. It is wise for the CCSM to confirm with the sales manager who is the main planner for the group. In addition this can change throughout the planning process if a third party is involved and if the main planner has additional staff working on different parts of the program such as rooms, food and beverage, audio visual, tradeshow, and so on.

Space Held but Events Not Listed

It's typical to have a contracted turned over with all space held on a 24-hour basis. This will show the meeting room name as listed on a 24-hour hold. However, the CCSM doesn't know what the space is being held for but it was probably communicated to the sales manager at the time of booking.

Therefore, the CCSM will not know prior to contracting the client if the space is for tradeshow exhibits, meal rooms, general session, and breakouts. This often won't present itself till the client sends their specifications to the CCSM. However, the production and audio-visual teams may know more initially than the CCSM.

Group Information, Profile, and History

Having complete group information will be most valuable in understanding how to address the needs of the group. Knowing demographics and average age of the attendees, where their meetings and events have been held in the past will assist with a CCSM preparing the entire hotel for excellent service.

CHAPTER 5

Communication: Listening and Delivering

Departments and Key Staff

CCSMs rely on several operational departments for successful meetings, events, conventions, and tradeshows. In catering conventions services a CCSM interacts with all departments with a hotel. Among these supporting departments are the following and their responsibilities and how this is vital to catering convention services support.

Sales managers and support departments:

- *Catering sales*: Typically, the first contact a bride and groom or nonprofit planner have—to build rapport and gain confidence their event will be a priority.
- *Meeting or convention sales*: They have the relationships and knowledge to convince planners your company is the right choice to earn their business and carry out expectations.
- *Group restaurant sales*: Provides groups that want a break from traditional meeting space with restaurant venues for meals.
- *Group rooms coordinators*: They are among groups' favorite staff for planner or meeting planners for all their efforts in the forever-changing reservations of guests, planner meeting planners, and their VIPs.
- *Business center*: This service can be an in-house offering or a retail lessee. CCSMs will work closely with the business center to inform meeting planners and guests of the services provided such as tradeshow outbound shipments, ordering of directional signs, making copies, mailing of all types, printing of boarding passes, and so on.

- *CCSMs*: Fellow coworkers with the same job title. This team is imperative to the overall success of the department. They provide mentoring, camaraderie, and relief when a CCSM is off work due to illness, vacation, meetings, and so on.
- *Front desk agents and managers*: Their duties are invaluable for finding solutions to check-in issues from early check-ins, late check-out requests, service recovery upgrades, and overall special room requests.
- *Housekeepers or GRAs (guest room attendants)*: This is the team responsible for cleaning all the guestrooms in the hotel. They are also the first to be accused of theft and the first ones to be praised for their abilities to turn a room from dirty to sparkling in a matter of minutes. Without a stellar housekeeping team the hotel will not have success, especially on days when there are an extremely high number of sleeping room check-ins and check-outs.
- *Convention setup*: This team is vital to the overall success in the timing of a group's general sessions, rehearsal and break-outs, setup of tables, chairs, staging, and so on. In casino properties this is a 24-hour, 7-day a week department with 3 shifts of staffing.
- *Banquet managers*: This team of managers and assistant managers are responsible for all food and beverage events on the convention floor. They coordinate with servers, food runners, and stewarding staff for the execution of breakfast, breaks, lunch, receptions, and dinner.
- *Banquet servers*: This team of dedicated staff is responsible for providing the actual serving of food and beverage to guests. This team works directly off the BEOs and under the direction of the banquet manager. They are compensated with automatic gratuity from a portion of the service charge. CCSMs work extremely closely with this team during the meal functions.
- *Stewarding managers and staff*: This team is responsible for the cleaning and polishing of banquet-serving items from china, glass, and silverware. CCSMs, chefs, and banquet managers

will work with this team advising during BEO meetings what equipment, size of plates, and types for glassware are needed for each event.

Chefs:

- *Executive banquet chef:* This person oversees most culinary operations including hot kitchens, Garde manger (*cold kitchens*), and pastry kitchens. CCSMs will work closely with this person to design custom menus, learning of food seasonality, cost, and unexpected shortages.
- *Garde manger:* This position is responsible for pantry and for the ordering and production of items in the cold kitchen, including items such as fruit, juices, salads, dressings, and cold hors d'oeuvres. CCSMs will work with them on custom items and special dietary requests.
- *Pastry chefs:* These chefs are responsible for the product ordering and baking of breads, pastries, desserts, and cakes. CCSMs will work closely with them on custom logo sugar pieces, unique desserts, and wedding cake design.
- *Chef Tournant:* These are chefs that support all kitchens and can provide answers to current stock for pop-up requests from groups needing food items not previously ordered.
- *Cooks:* They support all chefs and make up the most staff in banquet kitchens. This team works together to prepare food per the chef's instructions and gets it to the runners so all the banquet food is delivered on time.
- *Runners:* These culinary team members are responsible for delivering food from the kitchens to the proper ballrooms.

Engineering, facilities, or front of house departments:

- *Carpenters:* Lay dance floors, hang banners, build, fix, and maintain items in the hotel.
- *Electricians:* Responsible for the electrical power, air conditioning, fire watch, replacing light bulbs, fixing and

maintaining the electric fixtures and systems indoors and outdoors of a hotel.

- *Directors and managers*: Oversee the day-to-day operations within a hotel or facility. This can include the management of staffing, work orders, capital projects, fixing and maintenance of elevators and escalators, and hiring of specialty contractors and suppliers.
- *Bell desk and valet*: This team can respond to VIP requests including *room drops*,[1] group arrival via motor coaches, and wheelchair or motorized scooter rentals. CCSMs will provide these departments with group resumes, memo of local events that will impact the departments and the parking areas. In turn they control the hotel entrances with easy and professional coordination.
- *Room service*: Vital for the success of VIP amenity deliveries and coordination of meetings and catered events in suites.
- *Accounting*: This team provides financial accountability to the hotel. CCSMs will interact with them on contracted deposit collection, final payments, direct billing, aging reports, and final accounting.
- *Security*: This team provides for a safe environment for internal and external guests. They will also be the liaison with first responders, as well as local, state, and federal law enforcement when needed. CCSMs will work with them on notifying their department on issues within the meeting space and hotel that need their attention—items such as theft, unruly guests, medical emergencies, and crowd control. It's important to note that once a planner submits a written security report, for liability purposes CCSMs should not speak about this incident, but rather refer all questions directly to the security or risk management departments.
- *Human resources (HR)*: This department oversees all personnel issues. CCSMs typically will not work directly with HR, but

---

[1] Room drops: Amenities delivered to guest sleeping rooms, such as snacks, beverages or souvenirs.

their directors will in the hiring and discipline of associates. The team of HR professionals will also provide training to all hotel associates.

- *Risk management*: This department exists to minimize the legal responsibilities for the hotel. This includes putting into place programs or policies for safe working habits. CCSMs work with this department to obtain certificates of insurance listing the hotel as an additional insured for every provider of services that is in the convention space. Additionally, CCSMs will work with them on group special requests that may create risks within the meeting space such as demonstrations that are subject to potential accidents, use of exotic live animals, flying drones, and so on. Again, it's important to note that once a planner submits a written security report, for liability purposes CCSMs should not speak to this incident but rather refer all questions directly to the security or risk management departments.

- *Spa and fitness center*: This department is a favorite among hotel guests and may in fact be why they choose to stay at hotels that offer services such as massage, facials, saunas, and workout facilities. CCSMs will work with agents of these departments for making appointments for planners and their VIPS.

Wedding chapels: Some hotels, especially those in casinos, have standalone wedding chapels. Other hotels or facilities offer weddings in outdoor settings and inside ballrooms. CCSMs will work closely with wedding service coordinators on the timing of ceremonies as it relates to their corresponding wedding receptions.

Restaurants:

- *Group sales teams*: This team books group reservations with a set menu and food and beverage minimum. CCSMs will work closely with them on suggestion when a group is seeking a restaurant experience rather than a ballroom setting they have been in all day. This includes celebrity restaurants typically found in casino resorts.

- *Food and beverage management*: Managers responsible for staffing and the day-to-day operations of restaurants and bars. CCSMs will advise the restaurants via the resume of large groups that meals are not provided for. Restaurant managers are able to staff appropriately when hundreds of guests have a lunch break without a lunch provided in the meeting space.

- *Reservations*: An offering of the guest services, concierge, or telecommunication departments to take reservations when the restaurants are closed. CCSMs and their assistants are often requested to obtain VIP restaurant reservations for "C" level executives or meeting planners.

- *Marketing*: This team of professionals provides creative materials such as sales kits, property maps, and annual catering menus. Social media and its tracking is a large part of their responsibilities. This includes travel websites and their posting of guest experiences. Additionally, they provide TV, movie, special event and direct mail advertising for the hotel as a whole, and for individual departments. CCSMs will work with the marketing team on approving materials such as corporate logos, planners requesting the use of proprietary photos, filming within the meeting or convention space, special events, revisions to maps and menus.

- *Concierge*: This department may be in-house or outsourced to a private company. They provide reservations and recommendations for guests. These services include reservation and information on local restaurants, sightseeing tours, shopping, nearby medical facilities, and so on. CCSMs will be able to refer guests and meeting planners to the concierge for expert local knowledge.

- *Entertainment*: Hotels that offer in-house entertainment, such as casino show rooms, can also be of service to meeting planners. They can offer entertainment for general session and social dinners and receptions. This can include celebrity and local entertainers, DJs and even piano tuners. CCSMs can refer planners or schedule these types of service.

- *Retail stores*: Most hotels and facilities have retail components to their offers. These are stores such as clothing, jewelry, logo items, sundry items, and famous franchise or lessee chains. CCSMs will interface with retailers for suggestions to planners on request.

Unique to Casinos

In a casino hotel: CCSMs will be working directly with these departments:

- *Casino cage*: Vital for cash paid outs against master accounts.
- *Casino hosts*: Providing catering or meeting services to high-end casino planners.
- *Loyalty gaming card centers*: Referring guests to apply for gaming cards to earn points for hotel offerings.
- *Casino dealers*: This staff can have a very positive effect on convention or meeting guests by their friendly manner. The guests in turn speak of this experience to the fellow guests, creating a fun "free-time" environment.
- *Casino marketing*: This department is responsible for creating and executing special events such as New Year's Eve, 4th of July, slot tournaments, and annual major sporting events within the convention space.
- *Celebrity showrooms and nightclubs*: These hotels are popular for meeting planners to book parties and show tickets. They assist in the overall casino adult experience.

Internal and External Meetings Necessary for Coordinating Catering and Convention Services

Banquet Event Order Meeting

The objective of these daily meetings is to confirm the details of each meeting on a BEO to the operations teams and assign the overseeing banquet manager.

These documents are reviewed from top to bottom and left to right. This meeting includes chefs, banquet, and stewarding associates. The meeting starts with the director announcing:

- *BEO number*: Catering management systems automatically assign BEO numbers to each BEO. However, in large properties it is common to also assign internal numbers. This allows BEOs to be sent out in date and time order regardless of how many different groups have events on any given day.
- Each menu item in detail, including what type of plate will be used to serve each item. If there is a buffet, list plates, chafing dishes, cooking equipment, and so on, that need to be discussed.
- China, glass, silverware, linens, paper, and plastic to be used.
- Items to be preset by the banquet department or on food stations, bars and trade show or exhibit areas.
- Planner contact information and onsite contact details.
- Accounting information, such a group code.
- Room(s) setup information with number of tables and chairs in a specific arrangement such as theater, classroom, chevron, rounds, U-shape, conference, royal conference, hollow square, open, and cocktail style.

There are essentially two types of BEOs: (1) those with F&B (*food and beverage*) and (2) those with meeting or event room setup only without F&B. BEOs that include room rental, billing for keys, security, water stations, and labor are considered F&B BEOs because it is the banquet department that charges these into the internal systems.

BEO meetings are held every day Monday through Friday. The BEO meeting starts in the order of timing of events such as breakfast, followed by a.m. break, lunch, p.m. break, reception, and dinner. Once this is finished we start over with just the setup BEOs.

Small hotel properties and venues may conduct BEO meetings weekly or as needed.

Following are the days covered in a standard BEO meeting for large properties:

Monday: Wednesday BEOs are reviewed but first we review any changes for Monday and Tuesday.

Tuesday: Thursday BEOs are reviewed but first we review any changes for Tuesday and Wednesday.

Wednesday: Friday BEOs are reviewed but first we review any change orders for Wednesday and Thursday.

Thursday: Saturday and Sunday BEOs are reviewed but first you review any changes for Thursday and Friday.

Friday: Monday and Tuesday BEOs are reviewed but first we review any changes for Thursday, Friday, Saturday, and Sunday.

Those attending BEOs are key operations staff. These include:

- Executive director, director, or assistant of catering or convention services to lead the meeting (*If all are unavailable, a senior CCSM may occasionally lead the meeting.*).
- Each CCSM that has groups in-house with BEOs covering the dates being reviewed.
- Director of banquets or an assigned banquet manager or assistant manager.
- Banquet operations manager or assigned assistant manager.
- Executive banquet chef or assigned hot kitchen chef tourant.
- Garde manger chef or cold kitchen chef tourant.
- Executive pastry chef or assigned pastry chef.
- Executive steward or stewarding manager.
- Audio-visual manager or assigned representative.

If you represent multiple properties that operate as pods, a BEO meeting could potentially be reviewing multiple properties at a time.

The BEO is an extremely important document. It is the road map of the event. BEOs are covered more thoroughly in Chapter 6.

Preconvention Meeting or Pre-Con

Preconvention meetings are held a day to a few days prior to the start of a convention. These can be conventions of 10 to 5,000 rooms for large hotels. For *citywide* conventions, this could be in the tens of thousands of rooms.

The purpose of pre-con meetings is for planners and hotel operation teams to meet each other in a formal setting and discuss their roles for that particular convention.

Often the room setup for this is a hollow square with permanent nameplates for operations staff and temporary ones for meeting planners and their staff and vendors.

Guests of pre-cons can be, but are not limited to, the lead CCSM, director of catering and convention services, convention sales manager, banquet director or manager, convention setup operations manager, group rooms coordinator, front desk manager, hotel general manager (*for smaller noncasino hotels*), audio-visual manager, security manager, concierge, and spa manager (*if applicable*) on the hotel side. Planners may bring with them to the meeting: additional planners, third-party planners, outside audio-visual companies that travel with them, and exhibit, tradeshow, or drayage companies. It is essential that the planners advise the CCSM in advance exactly who will be attending the meeting.

The pre-con meeting is typically spearheaded by the lead CCSM for the convention. He or she will welcome the guests and introduce the main meeting planner, and then ask the planner to speak about the group profile and what to expect during the convention. Additionally, the planner may have their staff members introduce themselves and explain their roles of responsibility during the convention. Next the hotel operations team introduces themselves with each hotel staff expressing a welcoming message to the group, stating their name, position, and how they have prepared for the group. Each guest should have in front of them the group resume to review what is discussed in the meeting, for example early check-in, late check-out, off-site events, security and emergency procedures, and so on.

Depending on the planner's expectations and *hot buttons*, they may address items of importance to them such as *C*-level requirements, levels of service anticipated and whether they want to know challenges as they present themselves to help in their solutions rather than hearing about them after the fact. This is especially true for third-party planners. For example, if front desk check-in lines are quite busy we might recommend to the planners to suggest guests check-in via self-serve kiosks. Also, if a certain food item did not ship to the hotel in time, the CCSM lets the planner know and offers suggestions for substitutions rather than wait to see if they notice.

After these meeting formalities, the planner is invited to ask questions of the operations team. The lead CCSM will close the meeting with final announcements and invite certain guests to remain in the meeting room to review specific details such as guestroom reports, audio-visual changes, and full BEO reviews.

It is imperative that the planner sees, reviews, and makes any changes to the resume prior to the start of the pre-con. This is their time to confirm any changes they desire or any forgotten, missed, or noncommunicated information.

An important nontangible outcome of pre-cons is getting to see the planner's style and the rapport that's revealed and how to prepare for it. For example: Are they serious, humorous, nervous, anxious about a particular detail, confident in your service or experienced enough to know how to handle issues as they arise versus looking for a perfect and flawless event? By the way, in all our years in the meetings and convention business, we have certainly not witnessed a perfectly flawless event. Always *"expect the unexpected."*

Postconvention Meeting or Post-Con

The primary purpose of a post-con meeting is to gain feedback from the planner. This feedback generally will disclose how the hotel performed on all levels of service from the preplanning experience to the guest check-in to actual execution of events.

Guests of the post-con meetings are primarily the main event planning contacts and senior level hotel staff such as directors and executive directors of operation departments and general manager of medium- to small-size hotels. Note that planners may ask this meeting be held onsite, or they may prefer a conference call following the convention. Additionally, planners may follow up with written correspondence on their recommendations for future improvement. Occasionally they will ask for compensation for issues that were not resolved to their satisfaction.

Such items can include mistakes in overcharging for a particular item, food events or items that were missed, or perceived unpleasant service by staff.

It's a nice touch at post-cons to surprise groups with a champagne toast send-off and welcome them back for future events.

Resume Meeting

The purpose for a resume meeting is for all hotel operational departments to be briefed in person on a group resume (*typically, previously sent out in an e-mail distribution*) prior to the group arrival and pre-con. Typically, this is a regularly scheduled weekly meeting and covers group arrival 10 days to 2 weeks prior. During the resume meeting the director of catering and convention services will announce which resume is being reviewed and the CCSM for that group will verbally review each page of the resume and answer any questions that arise from the supporting team members.

Guests of the resume meeting are usually led by the director of catering and convention services, and include the following individuals:

- All CCSMs with group conventions for the following weeks
- Group rooms coordinator
- Housekeeping director or manager
- Bell desk captain
- Front desk manager

Also, based on the sales concession or group profile, specialty departments may occasionally attend, such as spa services, restaurant and outlet managers, and so on.

Resume meetings are a great time for the CCSM to communicate with the supporting departments about any planner nuances and items to be aware of that are not apparent from reading the resume—items such as: "*The meeting planner loves red wine and friendly housekeeping staff,*" "*CEO may have meeting planner secure motorized scooter, but doesn't want to be seen as helpless,*" and "*Group guests are not experienced travelers and may need additional explanation of hotel processes.*"

How Planners Annoy CCSMs

CCSMs have to juggle multiple events and myriad details on a daily basis. Planners can make their lives more difficult by doing any of the following:

- Failing to return e-mails or phone calls.
- Admitting extra guests to receptions that eat and drink, then refuse to pay for them.
- Expecting the caterer to deal with issues not included in the written contract.
- Insisting on more setup or teardown time than originally contracted.
- Walking in for site visits with little to no notice.
- Asking for a customized menu when they really just want a discounted menu.
- Adding extra meeting rooms that aren't contracted and not understand why there is a fee for this.
- Request special linen or chairs and not understand that the hotel has limited inventory.
- Requesting buffet props or decorations that are not available.
- Being cheap by ordering breakfast or break items by the piece and not ordering enough to supply the guarantee. This makes the hotel look worse than the planner because guests assume the hotel was being cheap.
- Waiting until the day of the event to give the hotel the *post as* for the various events. If the CCSM can get this information in advance it helps to communicate the group name to everyone.
- Using the hotel's capacity charts as the bible. These are usually guidelines based off minimal audio-visual or décor. If your setup needs are extensive you should have a diagram drawn to show how many guests you can really fit.
- Assuming there is an unlimited amount of dance floor. They cannot give every group a 30 feet × 30 feet dance floor.
- Assuming that cash bars should not cost the planner anything. We have to charge for the bartender and the cashiers.

- Failing to adhere to their approved banquet documents and making changes onsite, thereby disrupting the operations team staffing assignments.
- Assuming that beer, wine, and soft drinks bars should be materially cheaper than bars with cocktails.
- Using wait staff or setup people as servants. They can be very helpful, but they are not a planner's decorating staff or setup crew. They are there to serve food and beverage and make sure the room setup is done as per the specifications (*At union properties, staff are not required to assist in planner setup.*).
- Not complying with all of the details included on a BEO, which must be accurate and complete, including the guarantee, timing, vegetable plates, special meals, audio-visual, head table seating, and so on.
- Assuming that hotels are *not for profit* and trying to get caterer to reduce the price of food and beverage.
- Asking the caterer what the hotel is going to *give them* for bringing the hotel this great piece of business. Wanting something for nothing.
- Stalling on making decisions on menus, room sets, and so on. It takes time to prepare BEOs (*especially for large programs with many events*). If the CCSM doesn't have the necessary information they can't get the BEOs done, to the planner for signature, and back in time to distribute as needed.
- Dragging their feet on signing BEOs. It not only puts CCSMs in a bad position to have to hound the planner for signatures, but prohibits them from distributing the information in a timely manner to the culinary and operations teams.
- Allowing extra guests to attend an event, even when willing to pay for them. If more guests show up than the guarantee (*over the agreed upon over set*) it is likely there won't be enough seats at a plated meal, or enough food or beverage at a reception. If the CCSM tries to accommodate the additional guests, by adding seats, food and beverage, it makes them look like we weren't properly prepared.

- Intentionally under-ordering food. When ordering a la carte for an event, it is challenging at best when a planner intentionally under-orders food in order to save on costs. This is called low-balling. Many planners assume more food can be prepared if needed. However, additional food may not be on hand, it may take longer to prepare than the reception will last and makes the CCSM look like they ran out of food. The guests aren't aware of how the food was ordered so they often just assume the hotel didn't prepare enough.
- Not communicating what they need. Unfortunately, CCSMs are not mind readers. If you need a table for displays, awards, and so on, they need to know in advance. It takes time to get items out of storage and set them up properly. It also takes staff, linen, skirting, and so on, which may not be available at the moment you arrive, in a panic, because the room isn't set exactly how you need it.

One of the common threads is communication. Open lines of communication are imperative.

Do Your Events Stimulate the Senses?

We have five senses: smell, touch, taste, sight, and hearing. Are you using all five senses to stimulate guests at your events?

Smell

Smell can be a powerful sense. Smell is often our first response to stimuli. It alerts us to fire before we see flames. There are various types of smells, including:

Scent, perfume, bouquet, and *fragrance* refer to the smell of flowers. Be careful that the scent of the flowers in the centerpiece does not affect the palate and overpower the taste of the food.

Aroma usually refers to the smell of food. The smell of bacon frying, coffee brewing in the morning, popcorn popping—all evoke memories as well as anticipation.

Odor refers to bad smells, such as fishy odors, stale air in a meeting room, mildew, and so on.

Smell is more closely linked to the parts of the brain that process emotion and associative learning than the other senses.

Touch

Think of all of the different textures and temperatures you can feel. Order table linens with a good hand feel. They can be silky or velvety. Try using bubble wrap as a tablecloth. Guests won't be able to resist popping the bubbles.

Taste

This is a no-brainer. Provide delicious food.

Sight

Lighting can create a tone for the event and create a pleasing ambiance. There are all types of lights available, from tiny, sparkly Tivoli lights in trees to GOBO lights, that project images on walls, ceilings, or floors.

Colors evoke feelings. Reds and oranges are hot colors and excite people. Blues and greens are cool colors and calm people. Guests will eat and drink more in a brightly lit room with hot colors.

Hearing

Hearing is the ability to perceive sound by detecting vibrations. Pleasant sounds, such as music at a reception or dinner, can set a mood. Soundtracks of tropical birds or rainfall at luau type of events can elevate the atmosphere.

Staff Communications

Famed hotelier Ellsworth Statler (1863–1928) once said, "Hire only good natured people." What he meant was that you can teach someone a skill, but you cannot teach attitude. He espoused *service with a smile*.

In 2012, Cathay Pacific flight crews threatened a *no-smile strike.*[2] What a novel idea. Instead of disrupting service, they would be affecting the quality of the service. It would feel very strange to be in an environment where no one smiled.

After a long day of flight delays, waiting for baggage, standing in a cab line or being crammed in a shuttle, and sitting in traffic in all types of weather conditions, the last thing your guests want to encounter is a haughty front desk clerk.

Hotels have distinct personalities. Hotel personalities come partly from the décor and ambiance, but largely from the attitude of the staff that they encounter.

There is no excuse for poor service delivered with a bad attitude. Hotels should take the time to train their employees on how to develop a friendly tone of voice.[3] This is especially important for staff members that answer the phones. They need to *put a smile in their voice.*[4]

It has been said that people that smile while talking on the phone have a friendlier tone of voice. *Smile and dial* is common advice in sales and customer service training. Nestlé places a mirror at each phone rep station so the reps can see if they are smiling when they are talking on the phone.

Ritz Carlton teaches their employees that they are *ladies and gentlemen, serving ladies and gentlemen.*

---

[2] www.telegraph.co.uk/finance/newsbysector/retailandconsumer/leisure/9737387/Cathay-Pacific-crews-threaten-no-smile-strike.html

[3] www.wikihow.com/Develop-a-Friendly-Tone-of-Voice

[4] www.achrnews.com/articles/126561-the-importance-of-putting-a-smile-in-your-voice

CHAPTER 6

Food and Beverage: The Catering Part of Catering Convention Services Management

Catering in hotels and catering facilities is the creative side to this position. The possibilities for your artistic endeavors are endless.

To some planners catering is a necessary evil and regarded as forced offerings to meetings and conventions. Other planners enjoy being creative with their food offerings. These planners might be the type of person who enjoys cooking shows on television, following restaurant trends, an inspired home cook, and follower of celebrity chefs.

Also, some CCSMs are not always familiar or comfortable with questions about and the designing of menu items that are not on standard menus. They prefer to organize the group by way of their sleeping room block, VIP details, general session, breakout and tradeshow setup, and overall group coordination.

For the rest us, we love this part of the job! It allows us to keep the catering in our titles and expand upon it. Those of us that educate ourselves in food ordering, seasonal availability, preparation, trends, cost and pricing are comfortable working with planners and chefs to customize menus and price accordingly.

One of the first things to consider when planning a catered event is the reason for it.

Is the event mainly:

- to satisfy guest hunger?
- to create an image?

- to provide an opportunity for social interaction and networking?
- to showcase a person, product, or idea?
- to present awards?
- to honor dignitaries?
- to refresh convention guests and resharpen their attention?
- to provide a receptive audience to program speakers?

The CCSM should be informed about the reasons so that the appropriate menu and production and service plans can be created.

Typical catering food and beverage offerings during meeting and conventions:

- Breakfast: *including continental, plated, and buffet*
- AM break
- Lunch: *including plated, buffet, and box*
- PM break
- Reception: *stand alone or preceding dinner*
- Dinner: *including plated and buffet*
- Afterglow or midnight snacks
- Brunch
- Special events such as sporting and PR events

Breakfast

Breakfast is a functional meal. People are refueling after not having eaten for 8 hours or so. Speed and efficiency are important for the breakfast meal. This is especially true if the guests will be going to business meetings, seminars, or other events immediately after the meal. The last thing a meeting planner wants is to start the day's activities late and throw off the whole day's schedule. Everything must be ready at the appointed time in order to avoid this problem.

Many guests will skip the breakfast meal. Some of them traditionally do not eat breakfast. A few may prefer early-morning exercise workouts. Some may have been out late the night before and would rather sleep than eat. Check your meeting history so you know how many people usually show up and you can have an accurate guarantee.

Guests need to energize the brain cells. If they skip breakfast, chances are their attention spans will decrease and they will become irritable by 10:00 a.m.

The breakfast menu should contain energizer foods, such as fresh fruits, whole grain cereals, whole grain breads, and yogurt. In addition to providing a bit of energy, they are much easier to digest than fatty foods. This will keep guests awake and ready to tackle the morning's business.

There is a trend away from sweet rolls toward whole-grain, blueberry, and oat-bran muffins and fruit breads, such as banana or date breads. Sugary and fatty sweets, such as Danish, doughnuts, and pecan rolls, give only a temporary lift.

There must be some variety, though, at breakfast. While many persons will not eat sugary, fatty foods, they may want to have at least a little taste of one. As much as possible, the menu should accommodate all preferences. For instance, you can offer bite-sized portions of several types of foods on a breakfast buffet table.

A buffet is the best type of service to have for breakfast functions because it can accommodate the early riser and the late arrivals. In some cases, it may cost less than sit-down service. And it can be just the thing for guests who are in a hurry because, if there are enough food and beverage stations, a breakfast buffet can be over in less than 1 hour.

The traditional breakfast buffet includes two or three types of breakfast meats, three to six varieties of pastries, two styles of eggs, one potato dish, and several selections of cereals, fresh fruits, cold beverages, hot beverages, and condiments.

An English-style breakfast buffet usually includes the traditional offerings along with one or more action stations. For instance, an action station, where chefs are preparing omelets, Belgian waffles, or crepes, is very popular with guests. This type of service, though, can increase significantly the food and labor costs so it can only be offered if you are willing to pay an extra charge.

For the cost-conscious meeting planner, the more economical continental breakfast buffet is appropriate. The traditional continental breakfast includes coffee, tea, fruit juice, and some type of bread. A deluxe version offers more varieties of juices, breads, and pastries, as well as fresh fruits, yogurt, and cereals.

If a breakfast buffet is planned, you should make sure to separate the food and beverage stations so that persons who want their coffee quickly, or do not want a full meal, will not have to stand in line behind those who are deciding which omelet to order. You also should have separate areas for flatware and condiments, such as cream, sugar, and lemons, away from the coffee-urn areas. Since it usually takes a person about twice as long to add cream and sugar as it does to draw a cup of coffee, this type of layout will prevent traffic congestion. If separate beverage stations are not feasible, you should have food servers serve beverages to guests at the dining tables.

Conventional sit-down breakfast service usually includes a combination of preset and plated services. This is appropriate if the guests have more time and want to savor the meal a little longer. Served breakfasts make greater demands on the catering and kitchen staffs. More servers are needed and more food handlers are required to dish up the food in the kitchen. However, unlike buffet service, food costs are more controllable because you, not the guest, control portion sizes.

Many planners, especially corporate meeting planners, want some added luxury touches at breakfast. For instance, they often appreciate things such as mimosa cocktails, Virgin Marys, exotic flavored coffees, puff pastries, and fresh fruit in season.

Eggs Benedict are also a nice touch, sure to please the guest who is expecting a lavish breakfast meal. Eggs Benedict will hold up well without drying out, so are ideal for banquet service. Consider them for brunch as well as breakfast.

Many people are not very sociable at breakfast. Also, if the guests trickle in a few at a time, they might spread out in the function room so that they can be alone with their thoughts, or with their last-minute work. You should ask the caterer to make available newspapers, such as *The Wall Street Journal* and *USA Today*, to those who do not wish to fraternize so early in the day.

If a self-serve breakfast lasts 1 hour, be sure everything is replenished continuously, especially during the last 15 or 20 minutes. Many guests will show up at this time and expect the full menu to be available.

Here is a Pinterest board with breakfast ideas: www.pinterest.com/pattishock/breakfast/

Refreshment Breaks

Refreshment breaks usually provide beverages and possibly a snack. They also allow guests to get up, stretch, visit the restroom, call the office, check e-mail, or move to another meeting room for the next *break-out* session.

A refreshment break is an energy break. It is intended to refresh and sharpen attention. It also helps alleviate boredom that tends to develop when guests are engaged in tedious business activities during the day.

Refreshment breaks are typically scheduled mid-morning and mid-afternoon. They are usually located near the meeting and conference rooms. And they usually offer various types of *mood foods* that increase guests' enthusiasm to tackle the rest of the day's work schedule.

Ideally, the refreshment break station would include hot and cold beverages, whole fruits, raw vegetables with dip, yogurt, muffins, and other types of breads and pastries that will hold up well and not dry out. Chewy foods, such as peanuts, dried fruits, and sunflower seeds, should also be available because these types of products are thought to relieve boredom.

Water, soft drinks, and other cold beverages should be available for each refreshment break, whatever time of day the break is scheduled. Many guests prefer cold beverages throughout the day. Bottled water has become a very important amenity (*Bottled water is being replaced by water stations that are less expensive and more environmentally friendly.*). If each guest is allocated a reusable water bottle when they check in, they can refill it throughout the conference. The refillable bottle can be sponsored, so it can be provided at no cost to the planner.

Most of those who drink soft drinks prefer diet beverages. Experience shows that 50 to 75 percent of people selecting cold beverages will choose a sugarless drink, such as diet soft drinks, bottled water, or club soda.

Another major consideration is to locate the refreshment break station so that it serves the guests' needs. Ideally, it should be placed in a separate room or in the prefunction space. It should not be located at the back of a meeting room. If it is, a speaker will have a hard time getting started if guests are lingering too long around the food and beverage stations. The speaker also cannot compete easily with the food and beverage stations; guests are liable to sneak a quick trip to the back of the room and disrupt the proceedings. Furthermore, there may be unwanted noise when the stations are rolled in, set up, torn down, or replenished.

Be sure to know your glassware, cup, and plate sizes used at a refreshment center. A standard 12-ounce paper coffee cup or to-go cup, yields only about 10 cups of coffee per gallon. Most China coffee cups hold 6 ounces, so the expected yield would be 20 cups per gallon.

Another thing to monitor is cleanliness of the beverage area. A coffee urn or juice canister should have drip catchers set out under their spouts. Urns and canisters will drip a little right after a guest shuts off the spout. Provide drip catchers or the tablecloth will get wet and spotty. Drip catchers for coffee should have a few coffee beans inside; this will hide the drips, and as a bonus, will send coffee aroma throughout the area. For juice canisters, such as a lemonade dispenser, a few slices of fresh lemon inside the drip catcher will hide unattractive spills.

Since it takes twice as long to add cream and sweetener as it does to pour coffee, it is strongly recommended to have them located to the side so people have to move over to add them to their coffee and are not holding up the line.

Be sure to provide trash receptacles for waste and trays for used tableware. A server should be available to check the refreshment setup periodically and replenish foods and beverages as needed. He or she should remove trash and soiled tableware and not let them stack up. Someone also needs to be responsible for tidying up the break area regularly. Few things are as unattractive as finding, for example, a half-eaten pastry on a pastry tray next to whole, untouched ones.

Many planners, especially corporate meeting planners, want refreshment breaks available all day, so they can break *at will* instead of at a predetermined time. In effect, they want permanent refreshment centers. Meeting planners accustomed to conference centers expect permanent refreshment centers. Conference centers typically provide permanent refreshment centers, and if other types of CCSMs want to compete favorably with conference centers, they must offer similar amenities. Of course, since this type of setup requires a server to be constantly alert to fluctuating needs, a planner must be willing to pay the added cost.

You should offer all-day beverage service on your catering menus.

There are advantages to having permanent refreshment centers. Many meeting planners feel this will keep guests around all day. If guests go off to a restaurant outlet for a beverage, they may never return for the business activities.

A permanent refreshment break usually stocks coffee, tea, and cold soft drinks all day, and foods might be offered only at certain times, such as at 10:00 a.m. and 3:00 p.m. All-day neutral beverage service provides an attractive and comfortable social atmosphere for guests to congregate and discuss the day's activities.

Themed refreshment breaks are popular. The theme can tie in to the overall theme of your event. You can also look at the location of the event for ideas—a cable car theme in San Francisco, a Cuban theme in Miami and Elvis or Rat Pack theme in Las Vegas. Consider a seasonal theme— Baseball theme in October, Holiday themes, weather themes such as Winter Wonderland or Fun in the Sun, and so on.

Here is a Pinterest board with ideas for breaks: www.pinterest.com/ pattishock/breaks/

Brunch

Brunch is a late-morning meal that is eaten instead of breakfast and lunch. Often a buffet, both breakfast and lunch items are served. They typically include alcoholic beverages such as Mimosas or Bloody Mary's.

Here is a Pinterest board with ideas for brunch: www.pinterest.com/ pattishock/brunch/

Lunch or Luncheon

Lunch is a normally a lighter meal, usually eaten midday and is typically casual. Lunch is meant to offer a convenience to guests and to make sure that they will not wander away and disregard the afternoon sessions and meetings.

If a lunch is only intended to provide a refueling stop for guests, the menu should not include an excess of heavy foods. If guests eat too much heavy food they will probably become drowsy and inattentive later in the day. Heavy foods are greasy, fatty foods, as well as complex carbohydrate foods, such as rice or pasta dishes. These products take a long time to digest. Fats can sit in the stomach up to 12 hours or more. On the other hand, fruit and vegetables are digested more quickly. Complex carbohydrates are somewhere in between—they digest more rapidly than fats, but not as quickly as fruit and vegetables.

Working luncheons are often roll-in deli buffets that usually rely on white meats and salad greens. It serves the dieter, the man-handler, and everyone else in between. Heavy items, such as potato salad, should be served on the side so guests can take a small portion. Serving these heavy items on the side will tend to discourage guests from consuming too much. Sixty-four percent of Americans are changing what they eat to healthier food, according to a survey from the International Food Information Council.[1]

It is important to remember that guests may be eating several luncheons during their stay at the hotel, so variety is essential. Most guests are satisfied with traditional breakfast selections, but they normally seek a greater selection for lunches. Or else they may go to a restaurant or bar for lunch and be late getting back to the afternoon's business sessions. This may also throw off meal guarantees. Guests could get sidetracked and not come back at all. With working lunches, refueling, speed, and keeping guests on the property are the major objectives. The typical working luncheon is usually less than an hour.

The nonworking type of luncheon usually involves some sort of ceremony and is normally about one-and-a-half hour long. Many nonworking luncheons have speakers, audio-visual displays, fashion shows, awards, announcements, and so forth that may overshadow other objectives.

When you have a ceremonial type of luncheon, the logistics are more complicated. Head tables and reserved tables must be noted correctly, name badges prepared, audio-visual equipment installed and ready to go, all lighting synchronized properly, and printed materials, if any, set at each guest's place.

---

[1] Food Information Council: http://www.foodinsight.org/articles/2016-food-and-health-survey-food-decision-2016-impact-growing-national-food-dialogue

Buffet, preset, and plated services are the typical service styles used for lunches. Speed is usually a major concern. Consequently, menus and service styles are usually selected with quickness and efficiency in mind.

Many guests will invariably complain if it is not a hot lunch. While you want to serve a healthy lunch, you should have some fatty foods on the menu. Some guests will be disappointed if they cannot have a few French fries or a rich dessert. You should see to it that alternatives are available to satisfy everyone.

Box lunches don't have to be boring. If you are taking your group to an offsite location and providing a box lunch, look beyond the ubiquitous sandwich, piece of fruit, and cookie combo and ask the chef for more creative offerings.

Be sure you choose foods that go well together and don't make it some random assortment. Appearance is important, so pay attention to the color, texture, and taste of the food that you select for your lunch menu.

You can be creative and have lunch served in Japanese Bento boxes,[2] which are compartmentalized.

You can theme lunches to create a distinctive atmosphere, such as having Mardi Gras music playing as guests approach the room for a themed lunch. Everyone will literally dance into the room with big smiles on their faces. In Seattle, a Purple Haze lunch themed on native son Jimi, is a hit—not only for the music, but also for the themed menu that included a guitar-shaped dessert. Themes can focus on locations, seasons, upcoming holidays, and so on. You can have a tailgate party lunch for any sport.

Think of some fun and quirky theme dishes that will get people talking and go with the theme of the event.

Here is a Pinterest board with ideas for lunch: www.pinterest.com/pattishock/lunch/

Dinner

For many attendees, dinner is the main meal of the day, usually offered in the evening, and usually the heaviest meal.

---

[2] http://en.wikipedia.org/wiki/Bento

Dinner is the most typical catered meal for social, wedding, nonprofit events, and affiliated sponsored events. While it shares many similarities with breakfast and luncheon, usually it is longer and more leisurely in service time and a more elaborate affair. It is the largest meal of the day and can typically include an hour reception with alcoholic or bar beverages prior to the dinner and the dinner may include continued bar and added table wine service.

Dinner portions in catering are larger portions than breakfast and lunch events. It is important to have dinner menus on your catering menus that are larger in offerings but not identical to lunch menus. This is because planners will frequently ask if lunch menus can be served for dinner. This forces a CCSM to communicate to the planner *"yes, but at a higher price"* due to dinner portions being larger, the length of service time is longer and whatever else the CCSM can think of short-of saying NO.

If banquet dinner menus are as inviting, cutting edge and progressive as in restaurants, planners will be more likely to stay within the meeting space and to fulfill their contracted food and beverage minimums.

Dinners normally consist of multiple courses—anywhere from three to nine. Possible courses include:

- Appetizer
- Soup
- Salad
- Intermezzo
- Fish course
- Main course: *meat, vegetable, starch, bread*
- Dessert
- Cheese course
- Beverage

Unlike breakfast or luncheon, meeting planners are usually more adventurous when booking a dinner function because they usually have more money and time to work with. For example, Russian and French service styles are more likely at dinner than at other meals. Even the buffet, preset, and preplated service styles are enhanced. Also, award ceremonies, entertainment, and dancing are more common at dinner.

Many dinners are part of a theme, a fund-raiser, or other type of major production where food service is only one part of the event. Rarely are dinners scheduled merely for refueling purposes.

Dinner guests are not usually on a tight time schedule. They normally do not have to be at a business meeting or any other sort of activity later on in the evening.

Many meeting planners do not have sufficient culinary background or expertise to plan a major food and beverage function. We don't recommend prime rib with very large groups. It is difficult to serve rare, some prefer it well done, and once cut juices seep out and it loses heat rapidly. Likewise, you cannot do soufflés for large numbers of people.

Food must do more than simply taste good, it must also look good and be presented beautifully. We do truly eat first with our eyes.

About 15 minutes before you want meal service to begin, begin alerting guests. Start the music, dim the lights in the prefunction area, ring chimes, or make announcements to signal guests that it is time to enter the dining room and start moving to their tables.

Servers should be standing ready at their stations when guests walk into the room, not leaning against the wall talking with each other.

From serving to removing of plates, the salad course should take 20 to 30 minutes; the main course about 30 to 50 minutes, and the dessert should take 20 to 30 minutes. The entire banquet service will be about 2 hours for the typical dinner event.

A dinner usually is much, much more than a meal. Food and beverage is only one part of it. You need to work with a caterer who is able to juggle many attractions when helping planners plan these major events.

Here is a Pinterest board with ideas for dinner: www.pinterest.com/pattishock/dinner/

Menu Planning

Catering menus should be updated annually. This is much easier said than done. It's a good idea to start this process in July to have the menus ready for a December launch for preparing for the new calendar year in January. Unfortunately, you may be challenged with your January events using your previous year menus as the group planner may have budgeted based on the previous year's menus and have already made his menu selections.

Sometimes the perception of food is reason not to include it on your menus. Lisa Lynn recalls having Escolar fish on her catering menus and a planner not familiar with it researched it online and informed her it was referred to as a having a laxative effect. This fish was removed from the menus.

Failing to adhere to their approved banquet documents and making changes onsite disrupts the operations team staffing assignments.

The last few years there have been items such as hard boiled eggs, coconut water, and string cheese on break menus, beverages included in box lunches, and soup and salad combinations as a first course for galas dinners.

There are times when a CCSM and chefs will need to plan special, unique menus for custom events such as desserts for first courses and dining in the dark events.

The director of catering is often responsible for developing standardized menus (*in cooperation with the chef and the food and beverage director*), as well as unique menus customized for particular planners. The types of menu items a facility can offer depend on several factors. Before adding a menu item to a standardized menu, or before offering to accommodate a planner's particular menu request, the caterer needs to evaluate all relevant considerations that will affect the facility's ability to offer it and the guest's desire to eat it. Does the kitchen have the skill level to produce the item?

The demographics of the group attending the meal function must be considered. Average age, sex, ethnic backgrounds, socioeconomic levels, diet restrictions, where the guests come from, employment and fraternal affiliations, and political leanings can indicate the types of menu items that might be most acceptable to the group. Psychographics (*the study of guests' lifestyles and the way in which they perceive themselves*) can also be a useful indicator.

Age is often an excellent clue. Senior citizens usually do not want exotic foods or heavy, spicy foods, so excessive use of garlic, hot spices, and onions should be avoided. Avoid other distress-causing foods, such as vegetables in the cabbage family, beans, and legumes.

When a group is coming from a reception where heavy, filling hors d'oeuvres were served, the dinner should be lighter. If guests are coming from a liquor-only reception, then the meal could be heavier. If a group will be going to a business meeting immediately after lunch, order foods that will keep guests awake. Protein foods, such as seafood, lean beef, and skinless chicken, will keep guests alert. Carbohydrates, such as rice, bread, and pasta, tend to relax guests and put them to sleep. Fats, such as butter, whipped cream, and heavy salad dressings, also tend to make guests sleepy, sluggish, and inattentive.

Nutrition is a consideration for groups that will be at a hotel or conference or convention center for several days during a convention. Since virtually all meals during their stay will be consumed on the premises, special attention must be paid to nutritional requirements when planning menus.

Many people are avoiding trans fats, high-fructose corn syrup, sodium benzoate, and other unhealthy additives.

Whenever possible, have sauces and dressings served on the side so that guests can control their own portion sizes. Ask for fresh ingredients instead of processed foods that contain preservatives and other additives.

Menu Balance

When you plan a menu for a meal you should try to balance flavors, textures, shapes, colors, and temperatures. Appetites are stimulated by all of the senses. You should not plan meals that tend to overpower just one of them. Custom menus are becoming more popular, so it is important to be able to know what goes (*or doesn't go*) with what.

Color is pleasing to the eye. Be aware of how a finished plate of food looks; it should not be monochromatic. How appetizing would it be if the chef prepared a plate of sliced white-meat turkey, mashed potatoes, and cauliflower? Guests will be turned off by the lack of color contrast.

You also want to avoid colors that clash. A plate of red or orange pasta would not be the place to have a red or purple crabapple slice.

Be cautious of strong flavors that may clash or be too similar. You should not serve broccoli, cabbage, cauliflower, or Brussels sprouts at the same meal—unless you were serving a medley as one vegetable. They are all strongly flavored vegetables and are in the same vegetable family. You need more variety and contrast to create a successful menu. It is particularly important to serve a bland vegetable, such as a potato, rice, or corn, to counter one with a strong taste, rather than serve two strongly flavored or two bland flavored vegetables.

You should strive to have something mild, something sweet, something salty, something bitter, or something sour on the menu.

Textures also are very important. Ideally you would have a pleasing combination of crisp, firm, smooth, and soft foods.

Product forms, shapes, and sizes should be mixed and matched. You should offer as much variety as possible. For instance, a menu could include a combination of flat, round, long, chopped, shredded, heaped, tubular, and square foods.

A temperature contrast will also appeal to most guests. A menu should offer both hot and cold food options. If you start with a cold appetizer, you should then serve a hot soup, followed by a cold salad, then a hot main course. We like variety in temperature. Most people also like to have hot and cold together, such as a hot fudge sundae.

The preparation method provides an opportunity for several pleasing contrasts. An appropriate assortment of sautéed, broiled, baked, roasted, steamed, sauced, and smoked foods will be more pleasing to guests than will foods prepared only one or two ways.

Avoid the common mistake of serving two or more starches, except on buffets (*i.e., potatoes, rice, pasta, corn, etc.*). The word *starch* should never be printed on a menu. Starch does not sound appetizing—starch is for shirts.

You also should offer several types and varieties of food courses. A meeting planner should be able to select an appropriate combination of appetizer, soup, salad, main course, starch, vegetable, bread, dessert, and beverage from the menu offerings.

New catering menus allow planners to choose one from column A and two from column B, and so on, rather than having every item predetermined. This type of menu allows planners to choose a main course, types of vegetables, method of cooking, type of dessert, and so on. For example, a planner could choose to have the potatoes baked, au gratin, scalloped, or French-fried. This menu style should be limited to smaller properties. If you have five groups in-house and all order something different for lunch, it can be an operational nightmare.

Special Meals

There is more demand for special meals now than ever before. Guests come with all types of allergies, preferences, religious mandates, doctor's orders, and so on.

You should develop a procedure for dealing with special meal requests in advance. Last-minute requests can throw off the kitchen. Because they haven't planned in advance, they have to pull someone off of the line to work on one dish, which slows down the rest of the service. Most large hotels have breakfast potatoes and pastries on a daily rotation.

Always be sure the special meal is served last at each table. If it is served first, other guests may request that instead of the regular meal.

To simplify this process, request that the planner provides special meal tickets to those guests who request special meals during the registration process.

Some planners try to get reduced prices for things like vegetable or fruit plates, because they say a plate of vegetables costs the hotel less than that slab of prime rib. But, there is more labor involved in preparing and delivering a special meal. Special meals should cost the same or more than the regular menu. The extra labor and coordination are an expense.

To make life easier on the chefs, serving staff, and especially planners, do *vegan* meals such as butternut and acorn squash and risotto entrees. This satisfies most levels of vegetarian, vegan, and gluten-free requests. *Thrive Meetings & Events* will consult with hotels about providing special meals.[3]

Some planners will put a note on the registration form, asking anyone with allergies or disabilities to contact the planner so arrangements can be made. The National Association of Catering Executives (NACE) prints all menus in the registration packet with a form to submit if guests need any substitutions.

---

[3] http://thrivemeetings.com/

Menu design: Here is a Pinterest board with ideas for menus: www.
pinterest.com/pattishock/menu-ideas/

Special Diets

Guests with special diets will influence the types of foods served. Some
people cannot tolerate certain spices or peanuts (*allergic reactions*), sugar
(*diabetes*), salt (*high blood pressure, heart problems*), fat (*weight problems,
high cholesterol*), wheat, rye, or barley (*celiac disease*), or milk products
(*allergic reactions, lactose intolerance*).

Food allergies include:

- Gluten free
- Seafood and shellfish
- Nuts (*tree nuts and peanuts*)
- Eggs
- Cilantro
- Dairy
- Onion, garlic (*chives, leeks, and shallots*) all from the lily family
  of herbs
- Soy

An acute allergic reaction to a food may manifest as swelling of the
eyelids, face, lips, tongue, larynx, or trachea. Other reactions can include
difficulty breathing, hives, nausea, vomiting, diarrhea, stomach cramps,
or abdominal pain. Anaphylactic shock is a severe whole-body reaction
that can result in death.

Some guests consume special diets for religious or lifestyle reasons.
Some Jews require kosher foods; others may not keep kosher but will
not eat pork or shellfish. Some devout Muslims may only eat halal
(*approved*) foods. Some people will not eat red meat but will eat poul-
try and seafood. Many vegetarians (*often called lacto-ovo vegetarians*) will
not eat animal flesh but will eat animal by-products such as eggs and
dairy products, but vegans will not eat anything from any animal source,
including cream, eggs, butter, and honey. Accommodating some ethnic
or religious requirements may create added expenses because of a need

to hire outside-specialized personnel (*such as a rabbi to supervise kosher preparations*) or to acquire special food items.

Here is a Pinterest board with ideas for special meals: www.pinterest.com/pattishock/special-meals/

With enough advance warning, the hotel can order kosher meals from a kosher kitchen. There would, of course, be an extra charge for this. When it comes to kosher meals you have to be careful to ask: "*what level of kosher does the guest eat?*" (*Kosher style, Glatt, served with paper, plastic, etc.*). When doing events that are 100 percent kosher, you are at the mercy of the supervising rabbi and some are stricter than others. Lisa Lynn worked with one rabbi on a reception for 2,000 guests and he required her to order *whole salmon*—ungutted salmon that weighed a ton and were costly to ship.

Chef's Tables and Food Tastings

A Chef's Table is usually located in or near the kitchen of a restaurant. VIPs and special guests are served a special meal prepared and served by the head chef—often right in the kitchen. Some restaurants, such as Smith & Wollensky and Delmonico in Las Vegas have glassed in areas that separate the diners from the kitchen, while still providing a view of the activity of the chefs preparing the meal. Dining in this manner is pricey, but you may have a small group of important people that would love a unique experience.

Chef's tables are often used for tastings for high-end meeting planners that want to taste the different options available for the various courses. The tasting can be a degustation, which is a culinary term meaning an appreciative tasting of various foods. It focuses on the sampling of small portions of many of a chef's signature dishes in one sitting. Each course is presented in an Iron Chef format, where the chef describes each dish he or she has prepared.

A tasting not only allows a planner to decide between different items (types of appetizers, etc.) but also to test the food quality at the hotel.

Not every event will warrant a tasting. Planners with low budgets that are ordering ordinary items will rarely be given a tasting.

Some CCSMs try to avoid tastings, because many planners have abused the privilege by bringing too many people to the tasting. Realizing that many things are decided by committee, some CCSMs will provide a complimentary tasting for a set number of people, say four or six, but any additional guests will be charged a fee.

Belo Mansion in Dallas provides a copy of their tasting guidelines:

Tastings may be requested and scheduled for plated events with a food and beverage minimum of $10,000.00 or above. Availability of specific items to be tasted and scheduling of such tasting are at the sole discretion and availability of the Chef. Tastings are available Tuesday through Thursday, 1:30 p.m. to 3:30 p.m. This avoids any lunch or dinner events/ commitments with our Culinary and Banquet Team. Only one (1) tasting is offered complimentary for up to 4 people. We do not provide tastings for items from our stations and displays menus. We are happy to customize a menu to meet your style and needs or you may select from our selection of menus.

Provide us with your selection of:

- *4 Hors d'Oeuvres*
- *2 Salads*
- *2 Entrees*
- *2 Desserts*

Please forward three (3) dates and times that work best with your schedule, keeping in line with the above guidelines and we will find a date that works with our Culinary and Banquet Teams event calendars. We require no less than two (2) weeks' notice for such arrangements to be made. Lastly, we must have your menu selections no later than 10 days prior to the tasting to keep your original scheduled date.

Conducting a Food Tasting

Food tastings are often requested for events such as wedding receptions, nonprofit galas, large conventions with specific dietarian concerns and service level, and so on. Low-budget SMERF[4] meetings rarely merit tastings.

---

[4] SMERF: Social, Military, Educational, Religious, and Fraternal Groups. Typically low budget.

When planners book social events they often do this on blind faith that the food offerings will be to their satisfaction. Planners may take this blind leap of faith to book hotels and facilities, without having tasted their cuisine up to a year or a few years in advance, and hoteliers and other CCSMs therefore may provide a complimentary food tasting. It stands to reason that most CCSMs conduct menu tastings only after contracts have been signed. These tasting events are also a time for CCSMs to get to know the planner(s) on a more personal level and understand their preferences. It will also uncover important items such as allergies, religious and dietary restrictions, likes and dislikes of the planners and their guests, and families.

Weddings can involve just the couple or the couple plus each set of their parents. Tastings for a nonprofit gala can include the entire planning committee or board of directors. Corporate tastings are not as common but can be more grueling in their degree of critique, as these meeting planning planners may conduct tastings for annual conference at high-end hotels all over the country and perhaps internationally and compare those to yours. The CCSM is usually not privy to the planner's experience of what exactly went well and what didn't in food service and logistics at his previous conferences.

From a CCSM's point of view, the best part of food tastings can be their upselling opportunity by suggesting (*and providing tastings of*) added course food offerings such as soup, intermezzo, wines, cordials, and so on. Also, in the same vein, upgraded décor, linen, floral, lighting, and audio-visual can be suggested to the planner at this juncture. Lastly, the CCSM can actually get a head start on BEOs by the planner's confirmation of the food selected.

Food and beverage is generally the highest cost for many events. For planners to be able to experience the tasting of menu items before their event(s) provides them a sense of relief, an excitement of the upcoming event and allows them to make changes to customize the offerings.

Often the banquet and culinary teams will strive to *wow* the event planners attending the tasting with VIP presentations and serving equipment. And who doesn't like a wow? However, it's a really good idea to keep the tasting food presentation and serving vessels the same way you would be actually serving the group event onsite. This way the expectations were set and clearly understood at the tasting.

Tasting can range from a full menu with each course tasted by each planner and their guests to a sample tasting of each or selected items shared by all attending tasting. The planner will need to communicate which menu they are wishing to sample. For example, the plated, the buffet, or the food station reception items. For plated meal tastings it is appropriate to taste all items. For buffets and receptions it is appropriate to taste most if not all of the proteins, up to four hors d'oeuvres (*traditionally two hot and two cold, of which one of each should be vegetarian*), two composed salads, three entrees of which one should be vegetarian, and up to two desserts or three flavors of wedding cake. Items not feasible or necessary to try at a tasting are carving station items, cold seafood, crudité and cheese displays, salad bars items, action dessert station items, and most sides such as vegetables, rice and potatoes, and breadbaskets. A must try would be specialty desserts, signature drinks, and upsell of high-end varietal wines!

If planners want a more extensive tasting than you have proposed, it is absolutely appropriate to charge for the full price of higher-end items and the labor to cook and serve these items. Some facilities will credit back the amount of the tasting account after the event has actualized.

To save on food cost, a good idea is to present the items or entrée on a *show plate*[5] and then on a second or multiple plates divide the item into tasting portions and serve that to guests.

For the best results possible, create a tasting document and have that available for all those tasting to note their comments on. Also take copious notes on the planner's feedback, and photos of all items tasted and their presentation. E-mail and print these photos and distribute to the culinary and banquet teams both right after the tasting and a couple of weeks before the actual event(s). This will help any new team members to know what the planner experienced and is expecting for their event, which could be several months in the future.

Food Safety

According to FoodSafety.gov[6] one in six Americans will get sick from food poisoning each year.

---

[5] A decorative plate preset on the table settings and removed prior to service.

[6] www.foodsafety.gov/keep/basics/index.html

There is a difference between clean dirt and dirty dirt. Clean dirt is caused from everyday preparation and is removed every day. Dirty dirt hides in the crevices—it is dirt that is not cleaned up daily and it builds up. Dirty dirt contains bacteria and nasty creatures like salmonella,[7] clostridium perfringens,[8] or listeria.[9] And, food that is not handled properly can contain E. Coli.[10]

Is food kept at the proper temperatures? Perishable food must not sit out at room temperature for more than 2 hours. Foods must be kept above 145°F or below 45°F. The danger zone for perishable foods is between 41°F and 135°F. Temperatures should be checked both in the kitchen and in the chafing dishes that sit out on buffets.

Are food handlers wearing plastic gloves? Do they have their hair contained (*Back in the olden days, all servers, as well as food handlers were required to wear hair nets—not attractive, but effective.*)?

With outdoor events it is even more critical because there is not always refrigeration available, and foods sit out in the danger zone. Never have anything with mayonnaise, such as potato salad, or cream, such as a cream pie, sitting in the sun.

Receptions

At receptions, plates can add as much as 1/3 to food cost. Guests tend to pile food up on plates and often don't eat everything. Remember, it isn't how much they eat, but how much they take.

Pre-dinner receptions are designed to encourage people to get to know one another. Most conventions schedule an opening reception to allow guests to make new friends and renew old acquaintances. If a reception is not scheduled, guests may meet only the handful of people sitting at the dining table.

Stand-alone receptions are not predinner receptions. They are typically held during standard dinner hours and are intended to take the place of dinner. This type of reception allows guests more time to have

---

[7] www.cdc.gov/salmonella/
[8] http://en.wikipedia.org/wiki/Clostridium_perfringens
[9] www.cdc.gov/listeria/
[10] www.cdc.gov/ecoli/

a drink, eat a little, and get to know one another. Once a guest is seated at a banquet, they only have the other people at the table to network with.

The selection of food should include both cold and hot items. Food should have broad appeal. Here is a Pinterest board with ideas for receptions: www.pinterest.com/pattishock/receptions/

Determining Quantities of Food and Beverage

For receptions with dinner following, allow for about six to eight pieces per person. For receptions with no dinner following, anticipate approximately 10 to 14 pieces per person. If there are more females than males in the group, trend toward ordering 10 pieces, but if the group composition is the other way around, plan for 14 pieces.

Guarantees

Normally the chef will prepare enough food to serve more than the guaranteed guest count. This overproduction is necessary to avoid running out of food. If the menu includes unusual foods that cannot be used in other areas of the hotel or other events, the planner will need to pay a higher price to defray the extra food costs. With a standardized menu, planners may not have to worry about paying for overproduction. Chefs usually prepare for 3 to 5 percent over the guarantee, but this is negotiable.

The guarantee is critical. The planner must pay for the amount guaranteed, even if that many people do not show up. If a planner guarantees 500 people and only 300 show up, payment for 500 is still required. Payment for no-shows is called *attrition*. Generally, a planner gives an initial guarantee when the event is booked. A final guarantee must be made 48 hours in advance of the event, to allow the hotel to order the food and call in staff. In some areas, where food deliveries are not available on a daily basis, a 72-hour guarantee may be required. In some cases, hotels will allow planners to add additional guests as late as 24 hours in advance, but they may not subtract from the final guarantee.

Labor

Some menu items are very labor-intensive, particularly those made from scratch. This is particularly true of handmade cold hors d'oeuvres by the garde manger chefs. It is not unusual for labor costs to be as much as one-third or more of a meal function's total price.

Labor is expensive in the foodservice industry. There are many hidden labor costs that are not readily apparent. There is a great deal of pressure to hold the line on labor costs. To control labor costs, a hotel may need to purchase more convenience foods, reduce menu options, eliminate menu items that require a great deal of expertise to prepare and serve, or charge the planner more.

Beverage Offerings

Understanding the purpose of the beverage function will give the catering sales representative an insight to the type of event desired. This information is invaluable when creating an exciting, memorable event. There are many reasons to schedule beverage functions. These events usually serve as a way for guests to socialize and engage in networking. A short reception can provide a transition period from a long workday to an enjoyable dinner.

A cocktail reception scheduled from 6:00 p.m. to 8:00 p.m. instead of a dinner should offer a variety and quantity of foods so guests can have enough to satisfy their appetite.

Spirits include distilled beverages, such as bourbon, scotch, gin, vodka, brandy, rum, tequila, and a variety of blends. Spirits can be consumed straight (*neat*), on the rocks (*over ice*), or as highballs or cocktails, mixed with a variety of ingredients.

Trends show that overall consumption will average three drinks per person during a normal 2-hour reception period. Always consult the history of the group for liquor consumption trends. If the group history is not available, assuming that 50 percent of the people will order spirits, order the following quantities for every 100 guests (Table 6.1).

Wine consumption trends show that overall consumption will average three glasses per person during a normal-hour reception period. Assuming

Table 6.1 Par Stock for 100 Guests

Bourbon	2 bottles
Scotch whisky	2 bottles
Blended or Canadian	2 bottles
Vodka	3 bottles
Gin	1 bottle
Rum	1 bottle
Brandy or Cognac	1 bottle
Tequila	1 bottle

that 50 percent of the people will order wine, order 30 750-ml bottles for every 100 guests. Wine consumption trends also suggest approximately 60 percent of people will drink red wine, with the remainder preferring white.

Beer is classed as domestic or imported. Domestic beers would include Budweiser, Coors, and Michelob. There are also light beers, such as Bud Light, Miller Lite, or Coors Light. Imported beers would include Heineken, Corona, Fosters, Stella Artois, Pacifico, Tecate, Sol, or Dos Equis.

There are also specialty beers from microbreweries. Catering managers should know what is available in their area and be prepared to discuss these options with planners.

Kegs, or the smaller pony kegs, of beer would be appropriate for an outdoor tailgate, barbecue, or picnic, or where low price is a key factor. It is important to have the proper serving equipment and staff that are experienced with kegs so that warm or foamy beer is not served.

Neutral beverages do not contain alcohol and include sparkling or still water, tea, coffee, nonalcoholic wines or beers, juice, soft drinks, and so on.

Specialty Drinks

These primarily alcoholic drinks are a fun way to carry out the theme of an event. It can be by color, name, garnish, or presentation that makes these *must-try* event exciters. Still popular are anything-*tinis*. These are spins on the classic martini with items added like liqueurs and juices for color and flavor, for example Chambord, Grenadine, Campari, pomegranate, and cranberry juices for a red color. Other fun food items can be added for floating garnish such as mint leaves, cucumber and fig slices, assorted fresh and dried fruit skewered, or ribbons of a shaved vegetable on a large plastic pick. Lollipops and sugar swizzle sticks can be provided for stirring in sweetness.

Drink stations still in current popularity are:

- Margarita with flavors of strawberry, mango, peach, and so on
- Bloody Mary with gin, whiskey, bacon strips, large shrimp garnish, and so on
- Martinis with classic spirits such as vodka and gin or flavored spirits and garnishes
- Mojitos with various rums and herbs
- Mules from the classic vodka Moscow Mule to bourbon, tequila, fruits, and herbs
- Lemonade stand featuring flavored lemonade and a selection of hard lemonades
- Sangrias with seasonal fruit with red or white wines and nonalcoholic sangria
- Iced Tea with flavors of green tea
- Champagne cocktails and fruit puree Bellinis

Layering drinks for the horizontal effect can be dramatic. The trick to this is to know what liquids are the heaviest and should be poured first for the bottom layer. For example, one could start with Kahlua then pour a lighter liquid on top such as a banana liqueur, and top it with the lightest of the three such as Cinnamon Schnapps.

Search the Internet for sites on gravity charts[11] for layered drinks that list the weight and color.

---

[11] cocktails.about.com/od/mixology/qt/spirit_graudio-visuality.htm

Here is a Pinterest page with beverage ideas: www.pinterest.com/pattishock/drinks/

Liquor Laws

Liquor laws vary from state to state and even from county to county. Laws govern the times of sale, the days of sale, and the size of bottles sold. Delivery of any liquor must be provided by the hotel's contracted providers including donated products.

There are four types of illegal sales in all states:

- Sale to minors
- Sale to intoxicated persons
- Sales outside of legal hours
- Improper liquor license

Signage

One of the most overlooked components of creating specialty meals, buffets, signature drinks, and food stations is the appropriate signage. It is vital to the success of the event which you and the planner have created together to have signage that reinforces the theme. For example if you are serving a signature drink that is named *Trifecta* it's important to place a sample drink on the bar showing the three layers that correspond to the drink and how the drink fits theme of a horse-racing event. Then add the signage with the name of the drink followed by the ingredients list.

Group Cash Concessions in the Meeting Space

Another manner of providing a group with food and drink is through the use of cash concessions, wherein group participants *pay their own way* rather than being provided with these comestibles as a part of their conference or event participation. Planners sometimes view this as an easy way out, an efficient alternative that relieves them of making arrangements, menu decisions, and making payments to the hotel. This is usually requested by the planner for the hotel to offer, so they do not have to organize and pay for a catered function and they want to keep the guests close to the meeting space. Otherwise guests are required to find meals within the facility outlets or at neighboring restaurants where service times are unknown.

In actuality, cash concessions are generally a *lose-lose* proposition in view of the fact that most conference centers are not set up for this. In this case, cash food concessions can be discouraged by a CCSM in almost every circumstance, to eliminate added labor cost with little sales return.

The hotel loses because a cash concession operation is much more complex than it would appear.

- There are the logistics involved. The primary method of payment is cash, so cash registers are installed and power provided to them. In hotels or facilities where credit card payment is an option then POS electronic connections must be provided. Ropes and stanchions may be needed to isolate the food or beverage sales operation(s) from other convention users within the public shared physical space in which it is set up.
- Staffing is required to execute the sales transactions, bring in and later remove the products that are for sale. Whenever staffing is involved, labor and labor union rules and policies must be considered and adhered to. Servers and laborers are likely to belong to two or more different unions, which could create scheduling issues for more than one department. For example, if a hotel banquet facility does not have a cashier they need to request them from other food outlets such as restaurants, food courts, and so on.
- Finally, the concept of cash concession sales—particularly of foodstuffs—leads to considerable waste, since most all non-prepackaged edibles and perishable foods cannot be returned to inventory once they are placed on the selling table; the overages must be trashed.

The are times where cash concessions will pay off. These times are when the hotel may be hosting/sponsoring a several thousand person event where guests are held captive within the meeting space or an outdoor event for extended periods of time. For example, tournaments, pageants, sporting events and concerts.

The meeting planner loses because the hotel will contractually insist upon the cash concession operation returning at least a *bare bones* profit or breakeven return. Thus, the planner may be faced with a $3,000 (*plus or minus, depending on the nature of the meal and size of the group*) minimum charge, plus additional hourly fees for servers or bartenders. In their attempt to escape the complexities by using a less expensive, simpler solution, they usually end up paying for the service of providing the meal versus the actual meal for the guest. Also, the menu offerings are only what the hotel chooses to produce, which may be simple salads, a salad with protein, a cold sandwich, and prepackaged items such as chips, candy, energy bars, bottled water, and canned soft drinks.

And finally, with a cash concession operation, the meeting planner may have to pay for additional regulatory fees such as fire marshal permits and health department permit applications and inspections.

A very important part of safety is providing room layout diagrams in the fire marshal permit application process. Whoever submits the permit applications must show on their diagrams all items required by the local fire prevention department. This includes showing the dimensions of the egress, ingress, calculated amount of exiting, and all stationary and movable items in the room from tables, chairs, fire extinguishers, audio-visual equipment, registration desk or counters, ropes and stanchions, exhibit booths, food and beverage stations, and so on. Also, special permits may be required for motorized or gas vehicles displayed, certain types of cooking fuels and fire watch (*turning off the automatic sprinkling system*) for indoor cooking and theatrical hazing or fogging events. These permits will require plan checking approval based on diagrams and finalized by onsite inspections of code compliance.

The Banquet Event Order

How much attention do you pay to your BEOs? They should be read as carefully as a contract, because they are contracts and are legally enforceable. By signing the BEO, you are agreeing that the contents are correct.

BEOs are also called function sheet or event order. They serve as the basis of internal communication between departments. A BEO is prepared for each event and copies are sent to relevant departments, including the chef, the purchasing agent, the banquet manager, convention service management, and even the valet manager, so enough staff can be scheduled to park cars.

BEOs are usually numbered sequentially for easy reference. They are usually distributed one week in advance of event.

Pay special attention to the times and be sure they match the times on the guest schedule. Guests will be upset if they arrive for breakfast at 7:30 a.m., the time on the schedule, only to find nothing ready—not even coffee—because the banquet captain's BEO shows 8:00 a.m. as the start time.

Also check the room assigned. Hotels often switch rooms at the last minute.

Conducting a BEO meeting is covered in Chapter 5. A sample BEO can be found in the Appendix.

Elements of a BEO:

- BEO number
- Function day(s) or date(s)
- Type of function
- Planner name or signature line
- Planner address
- Contact person
- Authorized signature(s)
- Name of function room scheduled
- Start time of function
- Expected ending time
- Number of guests
- Number of guests to prepare for
- Menus
- Style of service
- Function-room setup (décor, table layout, staging, etc.)
- Special instructions (ice carvings, special lighting, dealing with entertainers, etc.)
- Prices, gratuity, taxes
- Master billing account number
- Billing instructions
- Reference to other BEOs or other relevant records
- Date BEO completed

- Signature of person preparing (or approving) the BEO
- List of departments receiving copy of BEO

Change order or change log: An addendum to a BEO. CCSMs or planners often make alterations to booked functions. They may order changes in the menu one week before the event is scheduled, switch from table service to buffet service three days before, or decide to add extra bars 24 hours in advance. Be sure the addendum is signed or initialed by both parties.

Resume: While a BEO is for one function, the resume is a packet of all of the BEOs for a multiday meeting, including room set instructions for all meeting rooms.

Specifications That Are Common for Large Hotel BEO Standards for 3-Hour Reception for 500 Guests with a 24-Hour Room Hold

All event lines should appear in time order followed by event name and then ballroom name for example:

12:01 a.m.–11:59 p.m.		Grand ballroom	*24-hour hold*
12:01 a.m.–4:00 p.m.	Set up	Grand ballroom	220 set (*total chairs*)
6:00 p.m.–9:00 p.m.	Reception	Grand ballroom	500 guarantee
9:00 p.m.–11:59 p.m.	Teardown	Grand ballroom	

Below this the food and beverage should be listed also in time order always beginning with cold items.

- *Seafood on ice displays*: Note number of pieces of each item
- *Cold food displays*: Fruit, crudités, cheese, and antipasto trays (*list number of displays*)
- *Cold hors d 'oeuvres*: Note if they are tray passed or stationary (*list number of displays*)
- *Hot hors d' oeuvres:* Note if they are tray passed or stationary (*list number of displays*)
- *Salad stations*: List types of salads and accompaniments
- *Hot buffet items*: List items in menu and accompaniments
- *Carving stations*: List types of meat followed by sauces and bread or rolls

- *Dessert stations*: List items in menu and accompaniments
- *Hosted premium bar*: List in order spirits, wines, beers, energy drinks, soft drinks, and bottled water

Notes should be made in the following categories:

Foyer Setup

- (2) 6 feet × 30 inches tables with VIP Covers, (4) chairs, (1) wastebasket for registration

Ballroom Setup

- See diagram—set by 3:00 p.m.
- Set 18 feet × 8 feet × 24 inches stage with (2) sets of side steps
- (10) 6-foot rounds of 10
- (30) low cocktail rounds with (4) four chairs each
- (30) tall standing tables

Audio-Visual

- Working directly with (*insert audio-visual manager and cell phone number*)
- List audio-visual if appropriate (*note many large hotels with outside audio-visual providers cover this on a separate contract*)
- Set by 1:00 p.m.—work with setup on timing of stage, table, and chair sets

Banquet Manager

- Tray pass hot hors d'oeuvres for first hour 6:00 p.m.— 7:00 p.m.
- Silverware in baskets at each station
- Use planner provided logo paper napkins at each station
- (2) stations for each food offering
- White underlay with black overlay on 6' rounds
- Black underlay with white overlay on low cocktail rounds and tall standing tables

Planner Providing

- (2,000) sponsored logo paper napkins

Chefs

- (2) stations for each food offering
- (2) chef attendants for carving station
- (1,000) pieces of hot hors d'oeuvres tray passed for first hour 6:00 p.m.—7:00 p.m., food stations following

Stewarding

- (2) stations for each food offering
- Induction tables for carving stations
- Heat lamps for hot hors d'oeuvres

Engineering

- Set 32 feet × 32 feet dance floor by 3:00 p.m. and *strike*[12] between 9:00 p.m.—10:00 p.m.
- Power to bars and carving stations

Schedule of Events

12:01 a.m. to 4:00 p.m. Setup
4:00 p.m. to 5:00 p.m. Band or DJ set up and rehearsal
4:15 p.m. to 5:45 p.m. Banquet server setup
5:45 p.m. Ready serve time
6:00 p.m. to 9:00 p.m. Guests enjoy food, hosted bar beverages, and entertainment
8:00 p.m. Soft close of any food stations and bars if needed
9:00 p.m. Hard close all bars and remaining food stations
9:00 p.m. Event ends

---

[12] Tear down.

Billing

Charge to master account #XYZ

A Common All-Day Small Meeting-Only Standard:

12:01 a.m.–8:00 a.m.	Set up	Ballroom A	U-shape for 30
8:00 a.m.–11:30 a.m.	Meeting	Ballroom A	
10:00 a.m.–10:15 a.m.	Break		
11:30 a.m.–12:30 p.m.	Lunch Break		
12:30 p.m.–5:00 p.m.	Meeting	Ballroom A	
3:00 p.m.–3:15 p.m.	Break		

Banquet Manager

- No food and beverage required—*meeting only*

Ballroom Setup

- See diagram—set by 8:00 a.m.
- U-Shape for 30
- Pads, pens, and mints
- (1) water station in back of room $250

Refresh Room

- 10:00 a.m.–10:15 a.m.
- 11:30 a.m.–12:30 p.m.
- 3:00 p.m.–3:15 p.m.

Audio-Visual

- Working directly with (*insert audio-visual manager and cell phone number*)
- List audio-visual if appropriate (*note many large hotels with outside audio-visual providers this is covered on a separate contract*)

Billing

Charge to master account #XYZ

General BEO Information

The standardized BEO contains six fields and will contain menus and items for a specific event.

BEOs need to be sourced and completed every Monday for any events taking place the following Monday–Sunday. Banquet manager must always be sourced. Any changes or additions made after this must be distributed appropriately.

Monday morning BEOs will be batch printed, copied, and distributed for the following Monday–Sunday.

BEO Types

1. Completed BEOs are in the system, checked complete, and ready to go for the weekly distribution. This will list the food and beverage order including number of expected guests and pricing, setup details, chef, and banquet manger notes.

2. *TBD (to be determined):* If you do not have the complete BEO information for a definite booking when the weekly is distributed a TBD BEO is sent out. List on this BEO the event(s) time, number of people, and event type and price. This will assist the banquet department in scheduling. Note that the banquet, setup, and culinary departments will schedule staff based on this information indicated. On the weekly, TBD should be hand written next to this information.

   Once the BEO is distributed *TBD* should be stamped on those BEO's.

   Please note that the banquet department will schedule staff based on the information indicated.

3. *Addition:* Pop-up events happen more often than we would like. Primarily this occurs because a group adds unexpected events. Sometimes it is because the planner didn't provide all of the correct

information, and sometimes because the planner did give us all the event information and we just couldn't get to it in time for the weekly distribution. Unfortunately, this causes additional staffing changes and additions that can cause undue stress on operation teams. However, in the hospitality industry we respond so quickly to these *pop-ups* that we have created planner expectations that we can make miracles happen onsite ... and they don't hesitate to request these types of unplanned add-ons! Pop-ups that happen during the day of occurrence, or within the next two days, warrant e-mails to the operations team. Pop-ups for the following week can go in the daily distribution for pop-ups.

4. *Revision:* Revision of a BEO should be used if a majority of the food, setup, or times has changed on an existing BEO. It is helpful to operations to indicate what your changes are. It is the discretion of the CCSM when to make to revised a BEO or whether to announce the changes at the daily BEO meeting. Once the BEO is distributed as a *Revision* a copy of it will replace the original in the BEO file.

   It is helpful to operations to indicate what your changes are. It is the discretion of the manager to make the judgment call on when a BEO is to be revised and redistributed or when the changes can be gone over in BEO meeting.

   Once the BEO is distributed, *Revision* should be stamped on those BEO.

5. *Change log:* It should be updated when you are making changes to a BEO.

   A change log should not be done when you are revising a BEO. These should be only minor changes such as adding a table, removing chairs, and so on.

   All change log changes need to be noted on the original BEO in the file.

Guarantee or Set

Guarantee and set numbers need to be agreed on at least three days (72 business hours) prior to the event.

Meal Types

Sample types of BEOs with general knowledge needed to create the correct BEOs.

1. If the group is under 25 people, continental breakfast and a buffet can go on the same BEO if the event takes place in the *same function* room (*coffee break staff*).
2. If the group is under 25 and the breakfast, lunch, or dinner take place in a *separate room* it needs to be on its own BEO (*only exception will be if the breakfast is continental*) (*A list staff*[13]).
3. Continental breakfast is considered to be an existing continental with one hot item regardless of size (*coffee break staff*).
4. Should two hot items be on the continental it becomes its own BEO (*A list staff*).
5. Coffee breaks and meal functions plated or buffet from 26+ need to be split on separate BEOs (*A list*).
6. Anything plated needs to go on a separate BEO (*A list*).
7. All plated functions go to A list.

Banquet Check Procedures

Most planners should be provided (either by the CCSM or banquet manager) with their banquet checks the following day of the event.

- Every day around in mid- to late-morning, the CCSM or banquet manager should present the planner with all their banquet checks from the previous day. This will allow the planners to compare the actual charges to their spreadsheet of budgeted charges or previously signed BEOs prior to actual consumption.

---

[13] The A list is the first group of banquet servers that are called in for events. Should additional servers be required, they would move to the B list, and so on.

- It will be each CCSM's responsibility to review the checks on a daily basis to make sure they are correct prior to delivering to the planner.
- In addition to reviewing the banquet checks the CCSM should review the micros check that will also be attached. You will need to double check the micros ticket to make sure that it matches the grand total on each of the banquet checks. This will also confirm this has been posted as definite revenue.
- If the checks have errors and changes need to be made, the CCSM will assure that the changes are made and the correct check is presented to the client.
- Once your group has concluded and all checks are correct the CCSM will notify the audit or the accounting department the group is ready for final billing as far as the banquet charges are considered.

Recording BEO and Banquet Check Changes

It is important that when the financial changes are made to the BEO that they are not only put into the change log, but *also changed in Delphi*, or another CRM system. The more correct the information is in Delphi or other CRM systems, the more accurate banquet checks and final billing will be at the conclusion of the event. Updating information with revenue changes will assist in monitoring the food and beverage minimum. Additionally, this will allow the CCSM to know where they stand for upsell incentives.

CHAPTER 7

Staffing and Service Styles for Food and Beverage Events

Service Ratios

Understaffed meal service is not compatible with successful events.

The cost of labor is staggering, so most hotels have staffing guides. The average ratio is 1 server for every 32 guests at a meal function regardless of the style of service, the type of menu, or whether the servers are responsible for wine service.

Service is critical. Many excellent meals are ruined by poor service. Meal service levels can run from 1 server per 8 guests to 1 server per 40 guests. Most staffing guides allow for 1 server for every 32 guests, but meeting planners often try to negotiate 1 server for 20 guests or 1 server to 16 guests, if there is poured wine or Banquet French service.

As with any negotiation, the planners need leverage. A low-budget group will most likely be required to pay extra labor charges. A high-budget group may be able to negotiate the charges away. Negotiation must take place *before* the contract is signed. As with any agreement, be sure it is in writing and signed.

For excellent service, the minimum service ratio for conventional sit-down meal functions with American-style service with some foods preset is 1 server for every 20 guests. If you are using rounds of 10, the caterer should schedule 1 server for every 2 dining tables. If you are using rounds of 8, 2 servers should be scheduled to handle 5 dining tables.

The minimum bus person ratio for a sit-down, served meal is 1 bus person for every 3 servers. If you are using rounds of 10, the caterer should schedule 1 bus person for every 6 dining tables. If you are using rounds of 8, 1 bus person should be scheduled for every 8 dining tables.

Some CCSMs will schedule one bus person for every two servers. This is usually done for functions that include several VIPs, or whenever the planner requests extraordinary service. Usually, you can make with one bus person for every three servers because servers normally are expected to perform some bus person work during the banquet.

If the sit-down meal function includes Russian, Banquet French, or poured-wine service, you normally should schedule 1 server for every 16 guests. You should schedule 1 server for every 2 rounds of 8, or 2 servers for every 3 rounds of 10. One bus person for every 6 rounds of 10, or every 8 rounds of 8, will usually be enough.

Regardless of the quality of a catered function's food and beverage, room setup, and overall ambiance, poor service reduces the guests' appreciation and enjoyment of the event.

Poor service will overshadow any other favorable aspect of the event. Guests will never be pleased if the service is lacking. They will usually remember a bad experience much longer than a good one.

Note: The number of servers available for any event can be affected by the number of *no-shows* on the day of the event.

Banquet Staffing

Breakfast: start time to 10:59 a.m.

- *Buffets*: 1 server per 40 guests (*two hot items or more*)
- *Plated*: 1 server per 25 guests

Lunch: 11:00 a.m. to 1:59 p.m.

- *Buffets*: 1 server per 40 guests
- *Plated*: 1 server per 25 guests
- *Box lunches*: 1 server per 150 guests (*no matter where the box lunch is consumed*)
- *Box Lunches*: 50 guests or less goes to coffee break servers, and 51 guests + go to A list servers

Dinner: 2:00 p.m. to end of function

- *Buffets:* 1 server per 40 guests
- *Plated:* 1 server per 20 guests (*marketing events 1 server per 25*)
- *VIP functions:* staffing will vary
- *Wedding plated or buffet:* staffing will vary

Reception: 2:00 p.m. to end of function

- 1 server per 100 guests
- VIP events staffing will vary on how VIP the planner is
- Wedding will vary per BEO agenda and food amount

Coffee breaks

- *Continental breakfast:* 1 server per 150 guests
- *Small coffee breaks:* 1 server per 3 functions

Additionally, it is important to note that banquet mangers may be overseeing more than one function at a time and the CCSM may need to be onsite to assist. This is especially true for detailed service events such as wedding timelines, where management is needed for coordinating grand entrance, champagne toast, and cake cutting.

What Is French Service?

There is some confusion on just what French service is. It is further confused by similarities with Butlered and Russian Service. Let's demystify the styles.

First, there are two types of French service—Cart French and Banquet French. Cart French is what most people are familiar with because it is most commonly used in fine dining restaurants.

Cart French service: The food is prepared tableside. Hot foods are cooked on a rechaud (*hot plate*) that is on a gueridon (*small table*). Cold foods, such as Caesar Salad, are assembled on just the gueridon. Servers plate the finished foods onto individual plates and serve them to guests from the right (*This is the only style of service where food is served from the right.*). Some foods, such as desserts, may already be prepared. They are displayed on a cart, the cart is rolled to tableside, and guests are served after making their selections.

Banquet French service: Platters of foods are assembled in the kitchen. Servers take the platters to the table where guests are seated. The server, using two large silver forks in his or her serving hand places the food on the guests' plates (*Now silver salad tongs may be allowed if the forks cannot be coordinated with one hand.*). Each food item is served, by the server, from platters to the guest's individual plates. Guests are served from the left. Anything that is added to a plate by a server after it has been placed in front of the guest—soup in bowl, salad dressing, sauce on dessert, and so on—is part of this type of service.

Butlered service: Foods are presented on trays, from the left of the guest. Servers make utensils available for seated guests to serve themselves (*This term is also used for butler passed hors d' oeuvres at receptions.*).

Russian (Silver) service: Food is cooked tableside, like Cart French service, except servers put the food on platters and then pass the platters at tableside. Guests help themselves to the foods and assemble their own plates. Service is from the left.

While Cart French service and Russian service both prepare food tableside, in Russian, the food goes on platters for the guests to select their own food, and in Cart French service the food is placed on individual plates before being brought to the table.

Butlered and Russian both allow guests to select their own food from a platter, but the platters are assembled in the kitchen for Butlered and tableside for Russian.

The Ever-Changing Buffet Versus Plated Meal Sell Price and Profit

Depending on the economic times and food cost, the profitability and price of a buffet versus a plated meal changes. The higher price of preparing more food on a buffet so you don't run out of any item is currently overall less expensive and more profitable than paying for up to 8 to 20 percent more servers for a plated dinner in terms of payroll, including benefits.

However, currently in some cities or states cooked food that is still in serving pans not yet presented to guests can, within certain restrictions, be donated to a proper licensed facility that arrives on property to take possession within a certain time frame and temperature of food.

It's a misconception that because you need fewer waiters it should be less expensive. Even though the number of servers a hotel has to staff at a buffet versus a plated dinner is only 10 to 20 percent fewer, the cost is a minimum of 30 percent higher that employer must pay in benefits for each server. In a union environment you would staff the same for buffet and plated meals. Buffet dinners also require the culinary team to prepare a much greater amount and variety of food, and as a result the culinary labor is much higher.

Action Stations

Action Stations (*also called Performance Stations or Exhibition Cooking*) are designed to provide a fun and engaging addition or distinctive alternative to the traditional dinner or buffet. Action Stations provide more flair than a traditional buffet, and they are more interactive than a seated dinner. This format encourages guests to move around the room and provides an opportunity to socialize and network.

Action Stations offer a unique experience, with live chefs preparing custom items while your guests look on! Many people do not like buffets, because they feel the food isn't freshly prepared. One of the best things about Action Stations is that guests usually get to choose their own ingredients and quantities to incorporate into the item and have it customized to their tastes. For example, at an Omelet Station, you could request ham and cheese, light on the ham.

Here are some ideas for stations:

- Flambé Stations for Steak Diane, Bananas Foster, Crepes Suzette, Cherries Jubilee, and so on
- Quesadilla or Taco Station with Fresh Salsa and Guacamole
- Fajita Station—Chicken, Beef, or Shrimp
- Oyster Shucking Station
- Sushi and Sashimi Station

- Steak Tartar Bar
- Asian Lettuce Wraps—Vegetarian or Chicken
- Russian and Domestic Caviar Station with Chilled Vodka
- Panini Station—Pressed to Order
- French Fry Station with Toppings such as Chili, Cheddar Sauce, Seasoned Salts, and so on
- Comfort Food Station with Meatloaf, Pot Pies, Mac and Cheese, and so on
- Southern Barbecue Station with a Variety of Regional Sauces
- Tomato Soup with Mini-grilled Cheese Sandwiches
- Grilled Pizza Station
- Chocolate Dipped Strawberries and other Fruit
- S'mores Station
- Crème Brûlée Station
- Cappuccino and Espresso Bar
- Mixology Station featuring Custom Beverages

Look for things unique to the area. In Hawaii, you could offer a Malasada Station (*Portuguese doughnuts*) or a Banana Lumpia Station (*like an egg roll with banana inside—a treat from the Philippines*).

While Action Stations usually cost more than a static buffet, guests love them. Be prepared for a per-hour, per-chef charge.

Action Stations are a wonderful way to bring food and entertainment together. Guests will be dazzled and delighted to see the sizzle and pop of the creative process.

To Speed Up Meal Service

While dinner can be a leisurely meal, breakfast and lunch usually need to be served more quickly, to allow guests to get back to the meetings and scheduled sessions.

Serving a continental breakfast is the fastest way to speed up service. A basic continental breakfast consists of a juice (*usually orange*), coffee and tea, and some type of bread (*bagels, muffins, toast, danish, etc.*). And, it is typically self-served. This also has a benefit of being more economical than plated, served meals. It is recommended to have hot pots of coffee on each table, so there are not long lines at a coffee station, which slows service.

Lunch normally takes about 1 hour and 15 minutes. If you want them out in an hour, you need to preset as many courses as possible.

The appetizer course can be preset, as well as the dessert. Or, the entire meal can be preset if you are not serving a hot main course. At one lunch everything was preset on mirrors the size of a placemat. The shrimp appetizer was up in the left corner, the chicken salad main course was in the center of the mirror, and the dessert was in the upper-right corner.

You should also schedule 1 server for every 15 (*or fewer*) guests.

You can also alter the normal way the meal is served. Typically, the servers will serve a course, wait for the table to finish, and then clear all of the used plates at once. When speed is essential, have the service staff serve each course, and clear each table as needed (*not waiting until everyone is done before moving on to the next course*). This will generally require additional labor, and it is not standard procedure, but rather a strategy to expedite the meal.

Six Types of Labor Charges for the Bar

Sometimes labor charges are included in the beverage charges, but often they are not. In most cases, the meeting planner will have to pay extra charges for bartenders, bar backs, cocktail servers, cashiers, security, and corkage. These charges are negotiable, depending on the value of the business generated for the hotel. If a cash bar sells over $1,000.00 in liquor during a reception, the bartender charge may be waived *if negotiated in advance*. But unless it is a very lucrative group, the CCSM will pass on the labor charges.

1. *Bartenders*: Usually the hotel has a policy that all beverage functions will need a minimum number of bartenders, or a minimum number of bartender hours, depending on the size of the group. One portable bar with 1 bartender per every 100 guests is standard procedure. If all guests are arriving at once, or if there is concern about them standing in long lines, 1 portable bar and 1 bartender for every 50 to 75 guests should be used. The total charge may be based on a

sliding scale. For instance, if 2 bartenders are scheduled, the meeting planner may have to pay something like $200.00 to $300.00 per 4 hours shift.

2. *Bar backs*: Normally, there is not a separate charge for bar backs. Their cost is normally included in the charge assessed for bartenders, because unless the group event is super large, the bar back will usually be taking care of other bars throughout the property. Typically, for every two bartenders, there is a bar back who helps them in replenishing ice, glassware, liquor, and so on.

3. *Cocktail servers*: Labor costs will increase significantly. They can cost as much as bartenders, so it's a luxury that can strain your budget. They may be unnecessary if you plan to have two or three portable bars set up throughout the function room and let the guests get their own drinks. On the other hand, if you have servers circulating the room with trays of poured wine or champagne, this will keep wine drinkers from clogging bar traffic and slowing down the beer and spirits service. You may also reduce consumption of alcoholic beverages if you tray-pass some of it. Like with butlered hors d' oeuvres, it's a tradeoff between product cost and labor cost. A server can usually make only three or four passes per hour through his or her assigned floor area. During each pass, he or she will usually be able to carry, at the most, 12 to 16 drinks. Count the time needed to take the order, wait for the drinks at a service bar, and to find the guests and deliver the drinks, it takes at least 15 minutes per trip. One cocktail server should handle 48 to 64 drinks per hour. This type of service is less efficient and requires more coordination and effort, and you often will have to pay for more bartenders to handle the workload.

4. *Cashiers*: Some CCSMs require a separate cashier, if for no other reason than to keep the lines moving. The meeting planner may eliminate this labor charge if he or she is allowed to buy drink tickets in advance and resell or give them to the guests; local liquor laws, though, may prohibit re-sales. Furthermore, if you try to add a little markup to the drink tickets' original price, there will be some unhappy people; however, you may be able to support that strategy if you are using the additional money to defray other costs, using it to enhance the money collected for a charity function, and so on.

5. *Security*: Depending on the type of property you are using for the event, you may be able to get by with the facility's in-house, licensed security team. This team typically patrols the entire property, so if the planner wants anything more they will have to pay for it themselves. The CCSM can usually arrange for extra security at the event; it isn't always necessary for the planner to hire an outside firm. But, there will be a cost.

6. *Corkage*: This is a charge placed on alcoholic beverages that were purchased elsewhere by the planner and brought into a catered event or a restaurant. It represents compensation to the food and beverage operation for receiving, storing, delivering, opening the items, providing glassware, and serving them. It is a necessary charge for at least two reasons; one, the hotel has to make up for the sales revenue lost by not selling the products—the more alcoholic beverages the caterer sells, the more profit made. And two, if the hotel charges something, then its insurance will cover liquor liability—a bonus for the typical meeting planner who does not carry that sort of insurance. If the liquor laws allow, and if your facility is willing, you may have the option of allowing planners to bring in their own alcoholic beverages. This is typically done with wines, especially unique wines that the planner has access to or only you can procure. It is also common if you have lined up a liquor distributor as a sponsor, who agrees to supply free wine for one of the meals or receptions held during the convention or meeting.

Beverage Service

One thing most receptions have in common is that they usually include alcoholic beverage service in addition to food. Another common trait is the fact that they are rarely scheduled during business hours; normally a reception does not begin before 5:00 p.m.

Receptions are often both social and business events. People love to socialize. Receptions provide a relaxed environment for networking, sharing, and bonding.

It's a little easier to estimate the amount of beverage alcohol you will need for a reception than it is to forecast food requirements.

If beverages are served, the bars and nonalcoholic-beverage stations should be spaced around the room. Place them at sufficient distances from the food stations so that people have to change locations in order to get a drink. This further increases mingling.

Liquor laws: These days it is very unusual for a beverage function to offer only alcoholic beverages. In many states, liquor laws will not allow alcohol to be served unless food is also available to help slow down intoxication. So, there will typically be at least a few hors d'oeuvres and dry snacks.

Liability: In view of increasing host and host-facility liability, you should not plan and purchase any event that offers only alcohol. They are socially irresponsible and ripe for liability lawsuits. The hotel and the meeting planner should never consider accepting this type of risk.

Par stock: Usually bars are set up with a par stock of beverages, ice, glassware, mixers, garnishes, and other necessary supplies about a half-hour to an hour before the event is scheduled to begin. The normal par stock used is influenced by the:

- Number of guests expected.
- Experience with similar events or group history.
- Amount of storage space available at the bar.

Your history is the best guide, but if you don't have a group history, Joseph E. Seagram & Sons, Inc. suggests that during the typical reception for 100 guests, 50 percent of them will consume 3 spirit drinks apiece.

Trends: Fewer open bars at receptions. Many companies that used to offer or sponsor these types of functions are not willing to be exposed to liabilities anymore.

CHAPTER 8

The Space: Choosing and Setting Up the Room, Outdoor Areas or Tents

Choosing the Room

First, a suitable event room must be selected in which to hold the affair. There are a number of things to consider when making this decision. The major factors are the appearance, location, utilities, and amount of floor space.

The dimensions of the room, the ceiling height, the number of columns, exits, and entrances, the proximity, number, and quality of restroom facilities, the colors and types of floor and wall coverings, sound insulation, and lighting are all critical considerations.

The overall appearance of the room is important. Consider the following features of a room:

Lighting
Sound
Color
Wall treatment
Temperature
Smell
Visibility
Layout

Columns are usually negative elements in a function room, because they can block sightlines for speakers or audio-visual presentations.

A lectern or head table should not be located near an entrance because the movement of those coming and going will disrupt the speaker. Be sure that the room is set up so the doors are off to the side so those arriving late do not interrupt the presentation.

Table placement at receptions also affects food consumption. An hors d'oeuvre table placed against a wall provides only 180° access to the food. A rectangular table in the center of the room provides two open sides and a full 360° access to the food, allowing greater food consumption.

Meeting planners should also be concerned with:

- Types of electricity available in house
- Types of electricity that can be brought in
- Maximum wattage available
- Maximum lighting available
- Number of separate lighting controls
- Heating, ventilation, and air conditioning (HVAC) capacity
- Internet access or Wi-Fi availability
- Closed-circuit TV, radio, and VCR system
- Closed-circuit audio-visual system
- Paging system
- Number, types, and locations of:
  o Electrical outlets
  o Electrical floor, wall, and ceiling strips
  o Phone jacks
  o Dimmer switches
  o Vents and ducts
  o Built-in speakers
  o Doors (*Do they open in or out? Are they single or double doors?*)
- If the function will be held in an exhibit hall, a meeting planner will also be concerned with the number, types, and locations of:
  o Gas hookups
  o Exhaust fans
  o Drains
  o Water connections

You need to consider several things when selecting the appropriate function room in which to hold your event. The major factors influencing the selection process are the ambiance, function room appearance, location, utilities, and amount of floor space.

Most hotels now charge room rental rates, which can only be negotiated away if the group is very lucrative. Sometimes room rental will be on a sliding scale, based on how much food and beverage revenue is generated.

Ambiance

Many people think ambiance means atmosphere. But, it is more than atmosphere. It is the feeling you get when you are in an environment, such as a meeting room. It is the mood of the room. It is affected by light, color, smell, sound, and other undefined elements.

Sometimes, the appearance of the function room will be high on a planner's priority list. Meeting planners are often attracted to a particular venue, especially a hotel or conference center, primarily because of the ambiance provided.

In Las Vegas, rooms that overlook *The Strip* are in high demand. At night, the view is phenomenal. Mountain and water views are also popular in many destinations. Many planners want to book these rooms regardless of any other advantages or disadvantages they offer.

The colors and types of floor and wall coverings are the first things you notice when viewing a function room. In addition to meeting fire and building-code requirements, they should be free from stains and in good repair. They also should be in good taste and decorated with style.

Guests tend to eat and drink more in brightly lit, colorfully decorated surroundings. Vibrant colors, such as brilliant red, hot pink, and bright yellow, stimulate the appetite. Dark tones dull the appetite. Examples of colors that cool the appetite are dark green, navy blue, gray, and black.

You should consider a function room's lighting and sound capabilities. If speakers are scheduled during the meal function, the room cannot have any dead space, *that is, area(s) in the room where sound is absent or unintelligible.* Lights should be controlled by a rheostat (*dimmer switch*) so the appropriate level of lighting can be achieved.

People gravitate toward natural light, which can warm up a room. The cold, harsh glare of fluorescent lights can negatively affect the ambiance of a room. While incandescent lighting is warmer than fluorescents, the best replicator of natural light is full-spectrum lighting.

Sometimes, when Patti is bored at an event, she amuses herself by looking up and counting the burnt out light bulbs in the chandelier. She also looks around to see if there are scuff marks on the baseboards or dirty carpets. These indicate to how well the property does with maintenance. If the room that guests see and eat in is not up to standards, they may wonder whether the kitchen is kept clean?

Many meeting planners are now doing their site inspections on the Internet, without even visiting the facility in person. You can't tell what a room is like by looking at pictures that may be outdated. And, you can't smell the room to see if the ventilation is good or if there are any odors or potentially mold.

If the function room directly abuts the kitchen, hallways, and service corridors, some action should be taken to prevent unwanted *back-of-the-house* aromas and noises from seeping into the function room. Employees moving about in these behind-the-scenes areas may occasionally cause distractions. Some guests may be unable to hear a speaker if employees are overheard shouting, laughing, or talking in the service corridor. Employees should be reminded to speak softly in these areas in order to minimize noise pollution.

Let There Be Light

Many meeting planners overlook the importance of lighting. Lighting can be the design focus of the event. Lighting can create a mood, enhance décor, or draw attention to a design element.

Warm white or light pink is a flattering color for people. Blue is romantic, but not flattering to the skin. Likewise green or purple can be unflattering. Only white light should be used on food or flowers.

Here are some lighting terms you should be familiar with:

Lighting Designer: Plans the lighting design, designs the light plot for the room, and creates lighting cues.

Lighting Director: Supervises on-site installation, makes adjustments, supervises the show, and programs final lighting cues.

Production or Lighting Company: Supplies light and sound.

Backlighting: Lighting behind items.

Dark Time: No one is allowed in the room.

Dimmer: Control over levels of lighting.

Lamps: Light bulbs or lighting fixtures.

Gels: Heat-resistant plastic film.

Uplighting: On foliage, plants, trees, and so on. *Do not up-light people.*

Accent Lighting: Draws attention to a specific item or area; can also use color.

PAR Cans: Stage rear and front truss.

Truss: Metal frames that lights are attached to.

Intelligent Lights: Moving and programmable.

- *Lekos*: Designed mostly for Gobos.
- *Gobos*: Stage, walls, floors, dance floor.
- Robotic Lights or Moving Lights:
  - o Can be programmed to travel all around the room.
  - o Fog is added to enhance the effect.
  - o More expensive; however, very dramatic.
  - o Can also add Gobos.

Room Dimensions

Ceiling height, number of columns, exits, and entrances, the proximity, number, and quality of restroom facilities, the colors and types of floor and wall coverings, sound insulation, and lighting are also important, especially for those facilities whose function rooms do not enjoy breath-taking views.

Function rooms that are long and narrow have a *bowling-alley* effect. This rectangular dimension discourages guest mingling, participation, and networking. It also affects service because many guests will tend to gravitate toward one end of the room. A bar at one end may be very busy, with the other bars having only a few guests. It is also difficult to place a speaker in a long, rectangular room, although it would probably be acceptable for the speaker to be midway on the long wall as opposed to either end of the room. The use of audio-visual is also limited in a long, narrow room.

Columns are usually a negative feature in a function room because they can block sightlines. This makes it difficult if there are speakers or audio-visual presentations during the event. A few columns are acceptable, but too many will detract from the event unless the caterer can suggest a room setup that will minimize their negative effects. For instance, buffet tables can be arranged between some decorated columns that may enhance the room's appearance. Or buffets can be wrapped around columns using hollowed out half-moon tables.

Usually a function room has a sufficient number of entrances and exits because a local fire code requires them. If you have speakers or audio-visual presentations scheduled, you will want to know how easy or difficult it will be to transport the equipment in and out of the function room. Some rooms have outside entrances and loading docks.

A lectern or head table should not be located near an entrance because the movement of those coming and going will disrupt the speaker. If a video or PowerPoint presentation is planned, plan to have the room set up so the doors are off to the side so a late-comer does not have to walk in front of the speaker and interrupt the presentation.

With audio-visual presentations, you need to be able to minimize the amount of ambient light (*i.e., unavoidable light seeping into a darkened room from around doors, draped windows, or production and service areas*) that can wash out the colors in a presentation.

Don't underestimate the importance of choosing the right room.

Space Planning

Local fire codes will dictate the maximum number of people who can be legally housed in a function room. Before making final decisions regarding room setup and aisle space, the caterer must check the local fire code for specific requirements.

Aisles allow people to move easily around the room without squeezing through chairs and disturbing seated guests. They also provide a buffer between the seating areas and the food and beverage areas. They are also needed for server access and maneuverability. Aisles between tables and around food and beverage stations should be a minimum of 36 inches wide. It is preferable to have 48 inches. The caterer should also leave an aisle around the perimeter of the room; while 48 inches is preferable, it should be at least 36 inches.

If the function includes dancing, the caterer can provide (*or rent*) about 3 square feet of dance floor per guest. If the caterer uses layout squares, most of these types of portable dance floors come in 3 feet by 3 feet (*i.e., 9 square feet*) sections; plan on using one section for every three guests. A 24 feet by 24 feet dance floor covers approximately 600 square feet of floor space; this would be sufficient for a group of approximately 200 guests.

For bandstands, estimate about 10 square feet per band member. Drum sets usually require about 20 square feet. Large pianos, synthesizers, runways, soundboards, and so forth need additional space. Disc jockeys will need space to hold their equipment. Check the entertainment contract as it may set forth the floor-space specifications.

Bandstands and other similar attractions are sometimes elevated on risers. Stage risers come in many shapes and sizes. Their purpose is to elevate speakers, other entertainers, or audio-visual equipment so that a large audience can see what is taking place at one end of the function room. Most risers are 4 feet by 4 feet or 4 feet by 8 feet. Folding risers can be adjusted to several heights. Risers should be set up with steps with attached handrails and light strips. A lawsuit can occur if a guest falls from an improperly set stage.

Space Needs for Sit-Down Meals

Choosing the right room requires knowing what you will need to fit into it. If round tables are used, you should allow about 12½ square feet per guest. This includes their portion of the table, plus the space the guest seated in a chair would need. Allocate about 10 square feet per guest if seating is at rectangular banquet tables. If round tables are used, about 12½ square feet per guest should be allocated. These estimates will be sufficient if the caterer is using standard chairs whose chair seats measure 20" by 20". Adjust estimates if smaller chairs (*seats measuring 18" by 18"*) or larger armchairs (*which usually have a minimum width of 24"*) are used. Round tables are the easiest for the staff to service and they maximize interaction among guests. Here is a Pinterest page on Meeting Room Sets: www.pinterest.com/pattishock/meeting-room-sets/

These estimates are for standard banquet chairs where the seats measure 20" by 20". You should adjust your estimates if smaller chairs (*seats measuring 18" by 18"*) or larger armchairs (*which usually have a minimum width of 24"*) are used. Round tables are the easiest for the staff to service and they maximize interaction among guests.

When planning aisle space, remember to leave enough entry and exit room for guests. You should plan to allocate sufficient cross-aisle space, *that is, aisles used for guests to collect and funnel in and out of the function areas.* A cross-aisle should be approximately 6 feet wide.

Cross-aisle space is very important when setting large functions. For a function requiring 100 tables, the CCSM should not set a square layout of 10 tables by 10 tables without allowing some additional aisle space for guests to maneuver comfortably to the middle tables from the outside perimeter. If you need 100 tables, you should set up four blocks of 25 tables. Within the 25-table block, 48-inch aisle space is sufficient. However, there should be a 6-foot-wide cross-aisle surrounding each block of 25 tables.

Before making final decisions regarding aisle space, the caterer must check the local fire code for specific requirements. In Las Vegas, the fire Marshall must check and approve any layout for 200 or more guests, because of major hotel fires in the area in the early 1980s.

For very large functions, a second dance floor is very convenient. Guests at the back of the room will not have to negotiate the long trail leading to the front where the single dance floor normally is located. But, this arrangement does divide the guests into two subgroups. Two dance floors placed as diamonds with the points abutting keeps separate dance floors connected.

Be sure the dance floor is safety-coated with an abrasive to improve traction. Be sure sections are flush against each other and there are no cracks in which a lady's high heel could get caught. All sides must be completed with trim pieces that slant and will not cause someone to trip.

If you are having a band play, estimate about 10 square feet per band member. Drum sets usually require about 20 square feet. Large pianos, synthesizers, runways, soundboards, and so forth need additional space. Disc jockeys will need space to hold their equipment; however, today's technology allows a DJ to work with a small computer and small speakers to generate a high-quality sound and an extensive catalog of music genres. You should check the entertainment contract as it may set forth the floor-space specifications.

Head tables usually need about 25 to 100 percent more floor space than regular dining tables. If the tables will be placed on risers, you must increase your space estimate accordingly to accommodate the platform area, steps, and the need to spread the table-and-person weight properly over the stage. For instance, if using typical platform sections measuring 4 feet by 4 feet and 4 feet by 8 feet, you would need to connect a 4 foot by 4 foot and a 4 foot by 8 foot to have enough space to accommodate a dining table measuring 3 feet by 8 feet. In other words, you will need about 48 square feet of platform space to accommodate approximately 24 square feet of dining-table space. The 48 square feet will accommodate four guests seated at 24-inch intervals. Twelve square feet per person is usually the minimum amount needed for head-table guests.

A raised head table for 12 people, plus a lectern, should be a minimum of 26 feet long. The rule of thumb is 2 feet per person, plus 2½ feet for the lectern. For more comfortable seating, allow 2½ to 3 feet per person.

If you have head tables reserved for speakers, dignitaries, or other VIPs who will be addressing the guests after the meal, you may ask the facility to set up extra dining tables on the floor for them, near the head tables, so they can eat without feeling like they are on display. Some people do not want to sit at an elevated table and eat. If there is enough space, they can eat at regular dining tables, and then move up to the head tables just before the program begins.

Setting up extra dining tables allows you to maximize the number of VIPs who can be accommodated at the head tables. For instance, if you have 10 VIPs and 10 spouses, you can set up 20 places at regular dining tables. Then, instead of setting up a head table for 20, you can set one for only the 10 VIPs. The spouses can remain at the dining tables after the meal.

Floor Space

To accommodate a reception adequately, allow about 5½ to 10 square feet of floor space per guest. With 5½ to 6 square feet, people will feel a bit tight; they also will have more difficulty getting to the food and beverage stations. Consequently, they may eat and drink less.

Seven-and-a-half square feet per person is considered to be a *"comfortably-crowded"* arrangement. It is thought to be the ideal amount of floor space per person for receptions and other similar functions.

Ten square feet provides more than ample space for guests to mingle and visit easily the food and beverage stations. It is an appropriate amount of floor space for a luxury-type reception. It is not an appropriate setup if a planner is paying according to the amount of food and beverage consumed.

Buffets

Remember to take into account space taken up by buffet tables, check-in tables, plants, props, and other décor when forecasting the number of guests that can be served adequately.

Buffet Layout

Buffet tables need enough floor space for the tables and aisles. An 8-foot long rectangular banquet table needs about 24 square feet for the table, and about 60 square feet for aisle space (*if the table is against the wall*); about 100 square feet for aisle space is needed if the table is accessible from all sides.

Allocate approximately two running feet of buffet table for each food container needed. To display three hot offerings, three cold offerings, and a condiment basket, set up a buffet table about 14' to 16' long. Two standard 8-foot rectangular banquet tables, will require about 48 square feet of floor space for the buffet table and approximately 150 square feet of standard 3-foot aisle space surrounding the buffet table. The total allocation for this setup, then, is about 200 square feet.

Buffets are generally faster and more efficient than table-service procedures, assuming that there are enough buffet lines to accommodate the guests quickly and efficiently. One of the potential disadvantages of buffets, though, is the possibility that some guests will have finished eating while others are still waiting in line.

Most meal buffets are usually set with one line for every 100 guests. This is based on the assumption that it will take 100 persons about 20 minutes to go through the line. One line is one side of a buffet table; if there are two sides (*double-sided buffet table*), this counts for two lines.

If the caterer sets one food buffet line for every 50 people, the caterer can feed the entire group in about 15 minutes. The first guest will take about 5 minutes to go through the line. After that, there will be about four guests passing through the line every minute.

Create an opulent look, using décor to make the table look bountiful. Create an illusion of excess.

Food Placement on Buffets

Lower cost food items, such as salads and breads, should be placed first on the table so that the guests' plates will be full by the time they reach the main course.

Buffet tables should not be set near doors or other entryways where they can cause traffic jams. If the buffet line will be longer than 16 feet, it should be two tables wide, *that is, about 4 feet to 6 feet wide.* A long, narrow line is unattractive.

If floor space is tight, ask the caterer to use double-sided buffet tables. They can save as much as 20 percent of available floor space. They also tend to reduce leftovers because, when service slows near the end of the meal, the caterer can close one side of the line and consolidate all foods on the open side.

Elevate Less Expensive Items

Put inexpensive food on tables with 360° access, such as vegetable platters or cubed cheese trays (*Cheese is extremely filling.*).

Tray-pass the more expensive items, such as shrimp, lobster, or beef wellington. Time the service so everything is not available at all times. First, tray-pass the shrimp, wait 5 or 10 minutes, then tray-pass the lobster, and so on.

There is so much plate waste with large portions. You would be amazed at how much food goes into the garbage. Food that has been plated and served or put out on a buffet cannot be donated to the homeless. Only prepared food that was not put out is accepted.

Buffet foods should be in smaller platters and bowls. Psychologically, people take larger portions out of larger containers. If you have a huge bowl of salad, when it is half empty it is not as attractive and still contains a lot of food that will be discarded, if not consumed by the guests. If that huge salad was divided into four smaller containers, that were replaced when emptied, that half that was not consumed was not out on the table, thus can be donated to the needy.

Here is a Pinterest page with examples, diagrams, and charts of buffets. www.pinterest.com/pattishock/buffets/

A hot-beverage station will need about as much space as a buffet table. Bars will need more floor space because of the need to store back-up stock, ice, and coolers to hold beer and some wines. Allocate enough working space for bartenders and, if applicable, cocktail servers. A small portable bar measures approximately 6 feet by 7 feet, or about 42 square feet. When considering the aisle and other space needed, allocate at least 150 square feet for the typical portable banquet-bar setup.

Room Layout

It is essential that CCSMs provide diagrams to planners and internal departments to be clear on the function room setup. Also this will need the planner's approval on the setup. This can be included on the Banquet Event Order (BEO). The BEO can also include designs generated by room layout software; these types of programs place tables, chairs, and other equipment into a meeting room. Room layout software can be downloaded from companies that produce and sell this type of software, such as:

- AllSeated www.allseated.com
- Social Tables www.socialtables.com
- Meeting Matrix www.meetingmatrix.com
- Room Viewer www.timesaversoftware.com

AllSeated is free. Meeting Matrix is integrated with Delphi, which many hotels use in their sales and marketing departments. The others provide a 30-day free demo period, then there is a fee.

Using facility floor plans and other schematic drawings that show square footage, dimensions, doors, and other factors may be important to the planner. Several visual plans can be developed using a basic template. There are many room size calculators online that can help calculate the amount of space needed. Simply Google "meeting room calculator" and you will find many options, including these: www.mmaweb.com/meetings/Workshop/roomcalc.html and www.mpoint.com.

The typical software program will draw a layout using industry standards as defaults (*which can be changed*) for such things as distances between rows of chairs or tables, aisle space needed, and the optimal angles that should be set to accommodate video presentations. Most of these software packages also will automatically generate standard seating styles.

There are samples of computer-generated floor plan layouts in the Appendix.

The tables used should be the standard ones whose heights measure 30 inches from the floor. The typical types used in catering are:

1. 60-inch (5-foot) round: Typically called a round of eight, or eight-top. It is usually used to seat 6 to 10 people.
2. 72-inch (6-foot) round: Typically called a round of 10, or 10-top. It is usually used to seat 8 to 12 people.
3. 66-inch round: A compromise table size, it is designed to take the place of the 60-inch and the 72-inch rounds. It can seat 8 to 10 people. If a caterer uses this table, the facility may be able to minimize the different types of tables it carries in stock.
4. Banquet Six: A rectangular table, measuring 30 inches wide by 6 feet long.
5. Banquet Eight: Similar to the banquet six. It measures 30 inches wide by 8 feet long.
6. Schoolroom or classroom table: Similar to the banquet six and banquet eight. It can be 18 or 24 inches wide and six or 8 feet long. It is used for business meetings where classroom presentations are made. Seating is usually on one side only. It can also be used as one-half of a buffet table. To create a conference table set, u-shape, double u-shape, modified u-shape, or hollow square, use a variety of 6 foot × 30 inch tables and 6 foot × 18 inch tables.

7. Serpentine table: An S-shaped table typically used to add curves to a buffet line. (*For interactive table discussions or group activities 6 serpentine tables with 3 chairs each can be put together to create a hollow circle for 18*). (See Figure 8.1 and 8.2 for a diagram and a photo using serpentine tables to form a hollow circle.)

8. Half-moon table: Half of a round table, or two quarter-round tables attached to make a half circle. Also referred to as a half-round. These are also used for sweetheart tables for two in weddings. This setup is used for couples not wishing to have large head tables.

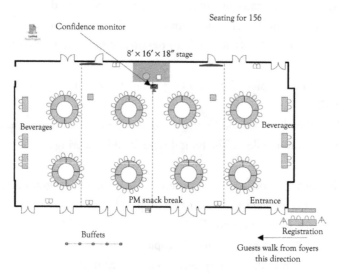

Figure 8.1 Graphic Room Layout with Four Serpentine Tables

Figure 8.2 Photo of Room Layout with Four Serpentine Tables

9. Quarter-moon table: A quarter-round table. It is generally used as part of a buffet line.
10. Cocktail table: A small, round table. It is usually available in 18-inch, 24-inch, 30-inch, and 36-inch diameters. Use 30-inch heights (*for sit-down service*), shorter tables (*for displays*), or highboy (*bar height*) tables (*for stand-up service*).

The seating arrangement used will depend on the purpose of the catered event. Awards banquets, celebrations, theme parties, and so forth will influence the dining-room layout as well as the type of tableware, props, napery, floral arrangements, centerpieces, and other decor used.

Renting Lounge Furniture

Most cities that host a lot of conventions have one or more furniture rental companies. You can rent all types of furniture suitable for indoor and outdoor events. If you want a lounge area on a terrace or cabanas around the pool or an intimate nightclub feel, the right furniture can set the mood, as well as provide comfort for the guests.

From sofas and chairs to huge Ottomans, you can rent from their existing inventory or have exactly what you want custom built. Just as with linens, you can choose from a variety of colors, prints, fabrics, and styles to match your theme.

You can use sofas and chairs on stage for panelists, instead of seating them behind a table.

You can add comfort and a softer look to hospitality suites held in function rooms.

The objective is to create an environment that will enhance the event. It is not just about furniture rental, it is about creating the right mood and ambiance.

Open-Space Seating

There is a trend to provide open-space seating at meetings, instead of just rows of chairs. People are of different sizes, they sit in different ways, yet there is a tendency to make all chairs alike. With open-space seat-ing you try not to furnish any room with chairs that are identically the same. Choose a variety of different chairs, some big, some small, some softer than others, some with rockers, some with arms, some wicker, some wood, some cloth. Put some highboys in the back of the room for people that prefer to stand. Have some tables, for those that prefer table seating. A furniture rental company can help you plan the space.

Open-space seating on Pinterest: www.pinterest.com/pattishock/open-space-seating/

What Is a Tablescape?

Tablescape is a term used to describe the tabletop. It includes the center-piece, linens, dishes, flatware, glassware, and any other décor. If you are on a tight budget and don't have much to spend in the way of décor, put your money in the tabletop.

Once guests are seated, the tabletop is their view for the rest of the event.

Tablescapes can set the mood. They can be themed to the event or the meeting. Pay attention to color. You do not want colors that clash with the carpet or other colors in the room.

The cover (*place setting*) should match the menu. For example, if you are serving soup, there should be a soup spoon on the cover. The bread plate, forks, and napkins are placed to the left of the plate. Knives, spoons, glassware, cups, and saucers are placed to the right of the plate. The dinner knife is immediately adjacent to the plate, with the blade turned toward the plate. The water glass should be placed above the knife blade. Wine glasses would go to the right of the water glass. If you are serving more than one type of wine, the wine glasses should be placed in the order they will be used. The first wine would typically be a white wine, so it would be furthest to the right.

Tablescape Tips

The dessert fork and spoon can be set above the plate, fork tines pointing right, spoon bowl pointing left.

Figure 8.3 Upscale Dinner Place Setting

Source: There are diagrams of table settings on this Pinterest board: www.pinterest.com/ tablescapes.

The bread and butter plate should be placed on the left above the forks and at about a 10 o'clock position in relation to the dinner plate.

There should never be a *naked cover*—which would be an empty space where the plate will go. You can fill the space with a napkin, a menu, a preset appetizer, or a show plate. A show plate is just that—strictly for show. It is removed after the guest is seated and before any food is served. A base plate serves as a base for several courses.

Cream soups call for a spoon with a rounded bowl, thinner soups would be served with a large oblong shaped tablespoon.

If you are serving salad, a smaller salad fork should be provided and set to the left of the dinner fork.

Fancier meals may call for small demitasse spoons, individual salt spoons, fish forks, or other types of specialty flatware.

You should have more than one set of salt and pepper shakers, creamers, and sweeteners on the table, as a convenience to the guests.

Cups and saucers should not be preset at a formal meal. It is often done for expediency, but they should not be brought out until coffee is served. And, the cup should never be turned over so the guest's view is the bottom of a cup.

Never place the forks on top of the napkin. The napkin should be placed to the left of the forks, unless you are using a fancy napkin fold in the center of the place setting.

Centerpieces

Centerpieces can greatly enhance the ambiance of a tablescape. They should never be at eye-level, which creates a disembodied voice coming from across the table when you can't see the person sitting there. Centerpieces should either be low, or elevated with a tall, slender epergne to *cap* the table.

Flowers should always be ordered a few days before the event so they have time to open to full bloom. While flower buds are beautiful, you want your flowers fully bloomed in all of their glory for the event. A beautiful floral tablecloth with a centerpiece made of the same flowers depicted on the tablecloth can make a stunning appearance.

You don't have to have the same centerpiece at every table. You can have a variety of different centerpieces around the room, which gives visual interest.

Edible centerpieces are popular. Appetizers or desserts can be displayed attractively instead of flowers. Baskets of assorted breads and breadsticks are always a welcome sight, because most people love good breads. Interesting centerpieces can be made from fruit or plates of petit fours. This Pinterest site has a collection of ideas. http://pinterest.com/shoppertwinmom/edible-centerpieces/

Some planners ask for centerpieces with *finger foods* on them when there will be an awards ceremony underway, "*so the guests can nibble while the awards are given out.*"

So, be creative and wow your guests at your next event.

Here is a Pinterest board with centerpiece ideas: www.pinterest.com/pattishock/centerpieces/

Choosing Flowers

Most people love flowers. There are ancient depictions of the giving of flowers in Egyptian, Roman, Chinese, and Viking cultures. We give them as gifts on birthdays, anniversaries, and other occasions. We grow them inside and outside of our homes. We wear them, and we even ingest them. They are beautiful, delicate, and usually smell good. The floral industry generates close to $30 billion annually in the United States.[1]

---

[1] Flower Industry Statistics: www.statisticbrain.com/flower-industry-statistics/

Most flowers are imported, with 64 percent coming from Colombia. The top fresh flower growing U.S. states are: California, Washington, Oregon, New Jersey, and Hawaii.

The best flowers for holding up for hours at events are roses and orchids. The most fragile are hydrangeas as they turn brown quickly, especially when blooms are handled by human fingers. For groups wishing to keep arrangements over the multiple days, recommend succulent centerpieces and indoor green plants.

Do you know how to choose flowers? Here are some tips:

- *Do the flowers draw water?* If flowers will be sitting for a while, or it is an outdoor event, ask the florist which flowers continue to draw water after the stem is cut. They will last longer.
- *Scent*: Do not put flowers with a strong scent, such as tiger lilies or hyacinths, into a centerpiece or anywhere around food. The scent interferes with the palate. And, some people have scent allergies.
- *Full Bloom*: Order flower a few days early, so they will be in full bloom during your event. Flower buds are nice, but you want the optimum display.
- *Eye Level*: Never order centerpieces that will interfere with the sight lines of seated guests. No one wants a disembodied voice coming through the flowers.
- *Seasonal*: Just like fruits and vegetables, flowers have seasons. Ordering local flowers, in season, is less expensive and better for the environment.
- *Meaning*: Different flowers have different meanings. You can find flowers that match the theme of your event. Or you can choose the flower of the month or state flowers for your location. About Flowers[2] has a handy guide.

Before choosing a florist, be sure they have experience and capacity to handle quantity production.

---

[2] http://aboutflowers.com/flower-a-plant-information-and-photos/meanings-of-flowers.html

Coffee Stations

Guests can draw 5 gallons of coffee from a single urn in 15 minutes; it is critical that the banquet team provide adequate and speedy replenishment. Anticipate 20, 6 ounce china cups or 10, 12 oz paper cups of coffee per gallon. It takes twice as long to add cream and sugar as it does to pour coffee, so cream and sugar should never be placed directly in front of the coffee urns. By placing these items away from the urn, the line will move much faster.

From left to right, items should be placed in this order to facilitate the traffic flow at a coffee station:

Cups, saucers, and to-go paper cups
Regular coffee
Decaffeinated coffee
Hot water for tea
Teabags, sugar, sweeteners, cream, lemon slices
Spoons or stirrers
Napkins
Food (*ideally this would be at the far end of a table, or on a separate table*)

The CCSM will arrange to place the items on the refreshment center menu, along with other utensils, plate ware, and silverware, on the other side of the food, or on the food table. Try to maintain easy access to the coffee urns.

Whenever possible, beverages, such as wine, hot coffee and tea, and soft drinks, should be served at the table for plated events. This provides a bit of personalized table service that guests appreciate. It also makes the overall service much quicker and more efficient.

Outside Events

Many events are held outdoors. Hotels often do events around a swimming pool or golf course. Whenever planning an outdoor event, an indoor weather back-up space must be held too.

Outdoor furniture can be rented to make a reception trendy and provide the comfort of a living room setting with sofas and easy chairs. Convention furniture rental companies have a wide variety of styles.

When using cut flowers in hot weather, avoid very delicate blooms, as well as camellias, gardenias and similar varieties that do not draw water.

Outdoor Checklist

- Are the sprinklers off? Be sure automated sprinkler systems are turned off to avoid soaking guests. Ask the site to avoid excessive watering for a few days prior to your event so guests do not sink into spongy ground.
- Has the area been sprayed for bugs? If insects could be a problem, have the area sprayed 6 hours before the event. If this is not feasible, advise the guests not to wear aftershave or perfume, which attracts insects. Perfumes are flower-based and attract all kinds of winged insects, including bees and wasps. Bright colors also attract bees. While it may be nice to hold the event in the middle of a flower garden, bugs and bees also find flowers attractive. The insecticide Pyrethroid is deadly to mosquitoes. For an environmentally safe pesticide, there is a fogger available that vaporizes an insecticide called Resmethrin, which is a low-toxicity pesticide that's people-friendly and has a less severe impact on the environment.

  Or you can incorporate sprigs of the citrosa plant into centerpieces and floral arrangements. The citrosa plant emits an odor of Citronelia that repels mosquitoes, but because of the odor, should be used some distance from food.
- Meat, especially if it is raw, attracts bees. If you are grilling steaks outdoors, keep them covered until they are tossed on the grill. When having activities outside, remember to be pro-active regarding insects, snakes and frogs or toads, and so on.
- Is electrical power available?
- Is there a back-up for inclement weather?
- If it is hot, misters help a little and a cover (tent) will help shield you from the sun, but not intense heat or humidity.
  o Misting fans are evaporative cooling. It is nature's own way of cooling the air.

- o Principle of *latent heat of evaporation,* heat is taken from the air to convert liquid to a vapor, providing a reduction in the ambient temperature.
- Consider rollups instead of silverware on the tables. If you put silverware out for a luncheon it may be too hot to touch by the time the event starts.
- With umbrellas, as the afternoon progresses, the position of the sun changes so the position needs to be changed periodically.
- Wind advisories: 20 to 30 mile an hour winds can blow over centerpieces and topple tables.
- Request that the lawn be mowed short, so that:
  - o The tables are level.
  - o The linens hang properly.
  - o Pesky mosquitoes do not hide in the grass.
- It can be too cold! Short receptions outside with a brisk evening can be ok, but there are times it is far too cold to have an event, and butane heaters have a very limited radius to keep guests warm. Butane heaters take the chill off of the air. They can be rented or purchased.
  - o If the event is by a pool, lifeguards are required at cost to the planner.
  - o Know that you do not have all day to set up your function as guests will be utilizing the pool during the day.
  - o Make sure to allow ample clearance around the edge of the pool so no one falls in. They may love the idea of lights strung over the pool, but glass is not allowed at pools.
  - o Offer alternatives such as battery operated lighting.

Dress Code

Planners should advise attendees of the dress code so guests know what types of shoes to avoid or if they should bring a sweater. A lady in high heels would sink into a grassy area. If some women will be in high heels, arrange the area so that part of it has a solid area, such as a sidewalk or parking lot. An alternative would be to lay out a portable dance floor so there is something solid to stand on.

Public Areas

When people want to have an outdoor function in a public area, they need to understand that while they may have their own area, it is not the same as a private indoor space. There are unavoidable noises that could affect an event such as natural noises, planes, traffic, emergency sirens, loud construction in the area, other guests, and music.

Lighting Is Key for Outdoor Evening Events

- Know when sun sets at the time of year of event to determine if lighting is required.
- Sunset is later in the summer, and sun glare is annoying.
- Be sure the guests will not be squinting into the sun.
- Note which areas will be in shade when you locate bars, buffets, and guest seating.
- This website shows sunrise and sunset times everywhere.

www.sunrisesunset.com/custom_srss_calendar.asp

Weather

When discussing outdoor events, you may want to mention when to make the call to move indoors due to inclement weather, usually 4 hours prior. That allows enough time to set the back-up space.

For an outdoor barbecue, check to be sure which way the wind will be blowing so it won't head directly toward the guests. When it is windy out, you can place a square overlay atop the table and knot the corners to hold the tablecloth down. Or you can use double-sided Velcro strips.

There are also Spandex table covers that cling to the table.

When food needs to sit outside, be sure it is shaded from direct sunlight. Never leave cream or mayonnaise-based foods sitting out. Bacteria can grow causing food poisoning.

On a hot day avoid foods that spoil quickly such as raw shellfish, mayonnaise-based items, or cream pies and cakes.

Humidity

Do not serve a hot, heavy meal on a muggy, humid day. Humidity wilts pretzels, potato chips, and cut cheeses. It also clumps salt (*In the South, they put rice in salt shakers so shaking will break up the clumps of salt.*).

To hold sandwiches over 3 hours:

- Use crusty bread and not sliced
  o ciabatta, focaccia, baguettes
- Use crisp lettuce or thinly sliced cucumbers
  o romaine leaves
- Use olive oil or vinaigrette
  o no mayonnaise
- Use hard, aged cheese
  o soft cheese melts
- Use cured meats
  o bacon, prosciutto, ham, salami
  o not fresh meat, such as roast beef or chicken
- Wrap them in thin, waxed paper

Beverage Service Outside

When chilling wine or champagne for an outdoor party, use the cardboard box the product was shipped in. Remove the champagne and cardboard dividers, line the box with two plastic garbage bags, then place the wine back in the box with equal parts water and ice. Cold water allows for a more rapid exchange of heat out of the wine or champagne.

Serving temperature can usually be achieved in 20 to 30 minutes, depending on the number of bottles, size of icing bin, and amount of ice and water. Only chill what you need. Bottles should not be left in the water indefinitely or the water will soak off the glue on the label.

Never allow champagne to get warm before chilling with ice. A sudden change in temperature may cause the champagne bottle to fracture with explosive results. Up and down of temperatures can lower the quality of wine.

Champagne corks are treated with lubricant for easy extraction. Warm conditions, such as direct sunlight on the bottleneck, will cause the lubricant to soften to a degree that will permit the cork to fly out of the bottle when the wire hood is removed. This is very dangerous and could cause injury. It is important to keep bottles shaded while the bottles are chilling.

Drape bottles with linen cloths to reduce exposure of the bottleneck to sunlight. The opposite effect is when bottles fall over in the iced water and become extremely cold. The cork lubricant hardens, making it difficult to pull the cork. Never remove the wire hood prior to uncorking the bottle. You can pull away the lead foil in advance, but always leave the wire in place, as it is holding the cork down.

Kegs of beer would be appropriate for an outdoor barbecue or picnic, or where a low price is a key factor. Ask for a keg counter. It will count the number of beers poured out of the keg. This is a good way to minimize theft.

See more outdoor ideas on this Pinterest board: www.pinterest.com/pattishock/outdoor-events/

CHAPTER 9

Nonprofit, Social, and Wedding Events: Understanding the Emotional Side of Events

Nonprofit Events

Nonprofit events are primarily for the purpose of fundraising for a nonprofit agency and its programs.

The key with nonprofit events is for the planner to understand that your business is *for-profit*. While catering and convention service businesses are quite benevolent and can donate some of their profits, they must cover food and labor costs.

Nonprofit groups can include a wide range of organizations to include but not limited to:

- *Medical*: research and development, patient assistance, health care centers, specialized education
- *Education*: sororities, fraternities, alumni, affinity school programs
- *Community Outreach*: human rights groups, animal advocacy groups, programs for the youth, elderly, disadvantaged, homeless, and the mentally, physically, and monetarily challenged
- *Religious*: from local churches to national programs
- *Media*: all kinds of reader- and listener-supported broadcast modes
- *Sports*: from youth programs to professional organizations
- *Tourism*: including the performing and visual arts, museums, aquariums, and so on

When these organizations hold their gala events they are predictably looking for donations of food, beverage, auction items, and volunteer services to attract high profile and affluent guests. Characteristically these events are evening dinner galas that include awards and recognition of community supporters. The higher the profile of the person being recognized, the more likely their peers or coworkers are to buy full tables to the event and spend money on auction items.

However, there are other community-based events that the masses can participate in such as walks, fairs, raffles, and sport outings to name a few. The primary focus currently remains on high-end dinner events.

Mainstream fundraising galas are typically three-course dinners with the first course often preset to allow for shorter meal service and more time for the programming. If timing is critical the dessert course can be preset as well. Most often table wine service is offered and the bar beverage is hosted by the planner. Food and beverage pricing is usually heavily negotiated during the sales and contract phase. The majority of nonprofits are certified tax exempt within the states where they reside.

When servicing nonprofit events, the CCSM can be tasked with working not just with one or two event planners but rather an entire committee of volunteers. It is important to establish a line of reporting to the final decision-maker and minimize the ordering around of the CCSM by volunteers.

This can be achieved best by experience with events of this nature and asking the questions in the early planning process. Questions like:

- Who will we be working with?
- Who is the decision-maker?
- Who is authorized to approve financial commitments?
- Can you provide a list of volunteers and their duties?
- Are meals to be provided for volunteers, vendors, and entertainment?
- Can we *all* meet for an onsite pre-event meeting to discuss expectations?

The actual event's success will in large part depend on the preplanning communicated on banquet event orders (BEOs). This must include all donated components and their pricing such as corkage and labor fees, all complimentary items such as votive table candles, waived bartender fees, upgraded linen, and so on.

Additionally, a detailed schedule of events should be made listing everything from setup timing, speaking and entertainment rehearsals, official opening time of event, food service timing, planner's items to be placed on tables such as table numbers and stand, name cards, menu cards, programs, and gifts. Service items such as wine glasses, preset food items, napkin fold style, linen colors for under- and overlays rentals such as chairs, charger plates, special tables, and sponsor name cards must be clearly specified.

Event planning items unique to nonprofit galas with silent and live auctions are:

- Planner's event theme and overall objectives
- Guest group profile
- Impact on the hotel such as early check-in, valet parking, and after-event plans at hotel outlets
- The setup of silent auction tables including locations, size, linen, décor, timing of setup and tear-down
- Dedicated areas and equipment needed for registration, auction check-out, Wi-Fi or hardline Internet for credit card terminals, volunteer needs, access to loading dock before and after event, outbound shipping for large items
- Entertainment and green room requirements
- Security provided by planner for auction items and audio-visual and stage sets the day or night prior
- Detailed floor plan diagram with table numbers, noted VIP seating, special meal requests and silent auction area; this may also include fire marshal approved plans
- Vendors
- Budgets are set early and will need to be constant monitoring and communicated to the planner

Following the event, surveys for planner satisfaction should be evaluated and the supreme measurement of your planner's happiness is annual repeat business.

What Happens to Surplus Perishable Food?

Do you feel guilty about the amount of food that gets discarded at the end of an event?

Today, programs have been developed around the country to collect and serve the food to the less fortunate in our society. Previously, hotels and restaurants had been afraid of liability issues and lawsuits if food were mishandled after leaving the kitchen and food poisoning resulted.

But, in 1996, *The Good Samaritan Act*[1] was created to prevent good food from being wasted and to shield donors from any liability. The Good Samaritan Act protects donors that donate wholesome food in good faith from civil and criminal liability.

The Environmental Protection Agency (EPA) has information on what kinds of food can be donated, where to donate, and liability information.

There are rules:

- Food that has previously been served to the public cannot be donated. That would include food sitting out on a buffet.
- Surplus food prepared in the kitchen, that was not set out or served can be donated.
- Refrigerated food must be kept at or below 40°F and frozen food must be kept at or below 0°F

Before you choose a food bank[2]:

- Be sure the drivers are trained to handle food safely
- Be sure trucks are refrigerated

---

[1] http://epa.gov/waste/conserve/foodwaste/fd-donate.htm (*You can download the Good Samaritan Act PDF from the EPA website.*)

[2] Atlanta's Table: www.acfb.org/about/our-programs/atlantas-table The Food Recovery Network: www.foodrecoverynetwork.org/ has a video about fighting waste and hunger by saving perishable food from college campuses. www.youtube.com/watch?v=QaKGr7u_Q1A Downtown Evening Soup Kitchen: www.downtowneveningsoupkitchen.com/donate/. Food Donation Connection: www.foodtodonate.org/ partnered with the National Restaurant Association. City Harvest: www.cityharvest.org/ has donation guidelines listed on their site. www.cityharvest.org/donate-food/donation-guidelines Feeding America has a Food Bank Locator, by state. http://feedingamerica.org/foodbank-results.aspx

Weddings

Great wedding planners are amazing human beings! They have the patience to handle a year full of couples and their family emotions and still deliver an exquisite once-in-a-lifetime event. These planners and their onsite teams are more than worth the financial investment made in them by the planner. A wise CCSM will work hand-in-hand with them and give up control of planning to them, thus being better able to concentrate on providing exceptional hotel service to the planner and *especially* the planners. Wedding planners may be guests under your roof, but treat them like family and they will increase your productivity and revenue!

Destination weddings are hot right now. And, Las Vegas is a prime destination.

Just about every hotel in Las Vegas has a wedding chapel and wedding packages. The Venetian in Las Vegas offers an Italian experience. You can get married in a gondola with a serenading gondolier on the Grand Canal or on the Wedding Bridge in St. Marks Square. Caesars Palace has a variety of wedding locations on their property, including classic and garden settings. Bellagio offers terrazza and courtyard ceremonies. Even the Circus Circus Hotel & Casino has a wedding chapel, which would be great if you are marrying a clown.

When people choose a destination they dive into the culture more than anything else. They have specific food and beverage that represents that particular destination as well as specialty entertainment. Also, people are choosing destinations where there are many things for their guests to do over the celebration of their wedding. Destination weddings are designed to keep people entertained, and, of course, tends to minimize the guest count which ultimately helps the couple save money.

When you work weddings, you either love them or run the other direction from them from fear of the emotional and sensitivity they bring to an otherwise conventional food and beverage event.

Of any event you can manage, weddings and wedding receptions are the most volatile. Planning these events, you see the best, worst, and most confusing of behaviors in people—from the bride and the groom, to the parents and step-parents, siblings, in-laws, and so on. This can include couples arguing in front of you, parents and children disagreeing on finances or number of guests or "*whose wedding is this anyway?*" disputes.

Divorced parents of one or both halves of the couple make it more complicated and bring up feelings of when they married each other. This doesn't sit well with their present spouse, often causing awkward public moments.

Successful wedding coordination takes patience, and the love of love.

Very few couples focus on the ceremony as much as they do on the reception and party aspect of the wedding events. When this happens, couples tend to demonstrate altar anxiety and actually shake in fear, especially the partner that didn't have much to do with the planning process.

Couples who display love and respect toward each other with joint planning duties have fun at their wedding. They have time to spend with their family and friends at their wedding occasion. Brides and grooms who tries to control the guests' experience rarely are relaxed and comfortable at their own celebration.

Couples attempting to control every movement of their guests will not be able to enjoy the spontaneity of what loved ones bring to the moment. This tends to happen when couples decide for the guests where to sit and who to sit with, what and when they can eat, drink, dance, and so on.

Your single most important focus in helping couples plan wedding events should be to listen to their wishes and reacting to them. Start this development process with asking questions about every detail.

Regardless of how many wedding events you have done professionally, and how you think you know everything about weddings, every couple is unique and should be paid attention to as if they were your first and only planner!

The next steps are bringing to the attention of brides and grooms (*or grooms and grooms or brides and brides*) what is the typical schedule of events and asking them what they would like their schedule to be. Ask questions such as: What song do you want the grand entrance to be? Who is announced at the grand entrance—just the couple or the entire wedding party? Is the first dance after the grand entrance, or after dinner? Is the Champagne toast given before the dinner to ease the nerves of those giving speeches, or after dinner when the risk of intoxication is higher?

Planning wedding ceremonies and receptions includes being knowledgeable about the following:

- Religious and ethnic beliefs, days of week and times of the day appropriate to have ceremonies, including receptions with and food and any beverage restrictions. For example, traditional Jewish weddings are on Sundays, East Indian wedding events may last three or more days and may involve riding large animals.
- Interracial, Lesbian, Bisexual, Gay, Transgender (LBGT), interfaith, nonfirst-time weddings, and those of persons with physical limitations may require additional knowledge on your part.
- Who is actually planning the wedding? Current trends are widespread when it comes to who is planning and paying for the wedding events.
- Are blended families involved in the events, such as stepchildren, honoring parents, and remembering those who passed on?
- Will any surprises need to be included in your timeline, such as an added event planned by one half of the couple for the other or parents for the couple, or guests' involvement? Often these are last-minute items that you must remain calm through and incorporate if you have a good sense the planner is in agreement with.

Additionally, wedding events take more coordination in the collecting and returning of planner's décor, program, and memorabilia items—such as personalized printed agendas, giveaways, table favors, photo booth accessories, cake toppers, cake cutters, name place cards, money card boxes, toasting glasses, and so on. It's always appropriate to advise brides and grooms wearing white to avoiding serving red wine.

Finally, wedding planners become attached to you and your knowledge. They want you to be there for most of their events. Often they will associate you with the beginning of their married life and want to stay in touch including celebration of their anniversaries. While these couples do not typically become repeat planners they will recommend you highly to others and try to reciprocate your hard work with testimonials and referrals. This is the ultimate compliment you can receive!

Table Linens

Once guests are seated, the top of the table is the view for the rest of the meal. Linens play an important role in creating the ambiance of a meal. Whether you use standard hotel linen, or rent upscale specialty linens, you should consider the color and texture that they add.

Linens for the table include:

- Table cloths
- Napkins
- Overlays and runners
- Skirting
- Chair covers and sashes

Color

Color is important as it sets the mood. Not only is it necessary to stay on top of the current trends in special event planning, but one of the first questions you should ask any planner is what colors will play a key role to the success of their function. And, as equally important, what colors are inappropriate, for example, a Chinese New Year party should never incorporate the color white! (*White is the funeral color in China.*)

Pantone[3] is the leading authority on color, and each Fall and Spring they announce the following season's color trends. Other color websites include: My Personal Artist,[4] The Perfect Palate Blog,[5] and Style Me Pretty.[6]

Type of Cloth

Standard hotel linen is usually Momie cloth, which is a cotton or polyester blend. There are many specialty linen companies that rent damask, satin, brocade, organza, lame, and even velvet linens. They also offer a variety of prints and patterns to fit every theme.

They can ship them from anywhere in the United States.

---

[3] www.pantone.com

[4] www.mypersonalartist.com/blog

[5] www.Theperfectpaletteblog.com

[6] www.stylemepretty.com

Table Linen Sizes

A 90-inch tablecloth for a 72-inch table (*Round of 10*), is recommended as it provides a 9-inch drop all around which should just graze the top of the chair. Floor length cloths for this size table would be 132 inches across. While floor length tablecloths look elegant, far too often the setup crew has pushed the chairs in too far, so the cloth does not fall straight. This ruins the effect that was intended by spending the extra money.

Party Rental Linens[7] has an excellent size selection chart that tells you what size tablecloths to use for the various sizes of tables, depending on how far you want the drop. A 9-inch drop would just graze the top of the chairs.

BBJ Linen[8] has a virtual design center on its website, where you can mix and match colors, patterns and styles of table linens. And, Creative Coverings[9] has excellent trend information.

Napkin folds can also set the tone of the event. Avoid napkins fanned out of drinking glasses. Lint can fall into the glass, and there is more handling of the glass, onto which guests place their lips. The Napkin Folding Guide[10] has many great folds with instructions.

Reception Food

Many receptions precede a dinner and are a way for guests to meet and mingle prior to sitting down at their tables.

Some receptions do not precede a dinner, are held during standard dinner hours, and are intended to take the place of dinner. Food should be heavier at these events because some guests will make it their dinner. You should offer a complete balance of food type, color, temperature, preparation methods, and so forth, to suit every taste. As this type of reception normally extends for a longer period of time than a predinner reception, people will in effect be consuming the equivalent of dinner, so sufficient backup food and beverage supplies must be available to prevent running out.

---

[7] www.lineneffects.com/size-selection.aspx

[8] www.bbjlinen.com/Design-Your-Event-Table

[9] www.creativecoverings.com

[10] www.napkinfoldingguide.com/

When planners order trays and bottles, they own the products and are allowed to use the leftovers for another event, or send them to a hospitality suite. When they order per-person, the leftovers belong to the hotel because planners are not buying a quantity of food or beverage, they are purchasing assurance that every guest will have something to eat and drink. With per-person, they pay to avoid running out; they don't actually purchase a set amount of food or beverage. The middle ground for the planner is to ask the CCSM to keep the food and beverage coming, and to charge for actual consumption. While they don't know upfront what their final cost will be, at least they won't run out.

The most important information in deciding how much food to order is the history of the group: Who are they? Why are they here? A pretty good determination can be made based on previous years. If this is a new group, or the history is not available, then consider the demographics of the guests.

As a general rule, guests will eat about six to seven hors d'oeuvres during the first hour. Guests will generally eat more during the first hour of a reception, but this depends on whether they are blue-collar, white-collar, or pink-collar (*demographics*).

White-collar workers are business types who are categorized by wearing suits and white shirts. Blue-collar workers are characterized as those who wear uniforms or work attire other than suits. Pink-collar workers are females in the workforce. Each group will tend to eat a certain way. It is safe to assume that a group of typical truck drivers would eat more (*and differently*) than a group of typical secretaries.

Here is a chart with some general guidelines that will help you estimate the amount of food to order for your group (Table 9.1).

For receptions with no dinner following, you should anticipate needing about 10 to 14 pieces per person. If there are more females than males in the group you can trend toward ordering 10 pieces, but if the group composition is the other way around, you should go for 14 pieces. Depending on the group, you should also consider ordering a carving station with beef, turkey, ham, or salmon.

For receptions with dinner following, you should allow for about six to eight pieces per person.

Table 9.1 Estimating Consumption

Type of reception	Type of eaters	No. of hors d'oeuvres per person
2 hours or less with dinner following	Light	3–4 pieces
	Moderate	5–7 pieces
	Heavy	8+ pieces
2 hours or less with no dinner	Light	6–8 pieces
	Moderate	10–12 pieces
	Heavy	12+ pieces
2–3 hours with no dinner	Light	8–10 pieces
	Moderate	10–12 pieces
	Heavy	16+ pieces

The selection of foods offered should include more cold items than hot ones. You should also have a crudités selection available. Food that is served should have a broad appeal.

You should serve foods that can be easily accessed by the guests and the food handlers who need to replenish the supply. Be careful when serving exotic foods that some guests may not recognize. If you are serving unusual fish items on a buffet table, you should identify them with signs in a font large enough to read in subdued party lighting. If unusual foods are tray-passed by servers; the servers should be able to answer any questions posed by guests.

Reception menu items should be bite-sized to allow guests to sample a wide variety of foods without wasting too much of it. It ensures that the foods will be easy to consume. Ease of consumption is very important since guests may have to balance plates, glassware, handbags, business cards, and cell phones while moving around.

Never tray-pass kabobs, baby lamb chops, or food with toothpicks, or other similar items. Once eaten, the guest is left holding a skewer, greasy rib bone, or annoying toothpick that must be discarded. They create slip and fall issues, create litter, and can later be found tucked down into potted plants, seat cushions, and other hiding places.

Foods should not be messy or greasy and they should not leave stains on clothes or teeth. Be careful not to order oversauced foods, such as barbecued chicken wings, that might drip when guests are eating them.

A better choice would be boneless chicken tenders that are lightly coated or served with a stiff sauce on the side.

You should always place salt and pepper shakers at carving stations. There are often a lot of other condiments set out, but rarely salt and pepper. A lot of people like salt on their meat or else they find it tasteless. It is a good idea to list salt and pepper on the BEO.

As even small plates may increase your cost by over one-third, be particularly certain not to use dinner-sized plates for receptions. Plates encourage overeating and excessive waste because a guest may fill the plate, eat some of the food, set the plate down somewhere, forget it, and then go back for another plate of food. It is not what quantity people eat; it's how much they put on their plate. Another disadvantage of using plates: guests with plates full of food will try to find a place to sit down to eat and will not mingle and network very much, if at all.

To encourage mingling, and to control food costs, you could have servers passing foods in addition to, or instead of, placing food buffet stations throughout the room. Guests tend to eat less if the foods are passed. Generally speaking, if the foods are displayed on a buffet table where guests can help themselves, they will eat twice as much as they would if all foods were passed butler-style by servers. You would want to compare the savings with the extra labor cost, though, before making this decision.

Usually you would not have all foods passed, although it is easier to retain control of food quantities by pacing quantities, balancing expensive items with low-priced items, and avoiding the food excesses that buffets require. Generally, at least one or two food stations or action stations will enhance the visual appearance of the function room. To save money, expensive items could be passed, and inexpensive food (*such as cheese cubes, vegetable trays, and dry snacks*) could be available on tables. A meeting planner without budgetary concerns would probably prefer guests to have access to a mountain of shrimp on ice and a sliced tenderloin action station.

If you offer butlered foods, you should place only one type of food on a tray, or guests will take too long to make their selections. If they cannot decide easily what to take, they may take one of each. This will slow down service because the servers will not be able to work the room quickly and efficiently. It also might encourage overconsumption and food waste.

Butlered food should always be *finger food*—food that can be consumed without eating utensils. The server should always carry a small stack of cocktail napkins.

With butlered service, the labor charge will be a bit higher. This should be offset with a lower food cost. Guests will consume less if foods are passed. You also can control the pace of service. You can stagger service by having servers with trays sent out every 15 minutes instead of taking all the food out at one time. Passed foods lend an air of elegance to the reception that many guests will appreciate. Be sure servers are assigned areas of the room to cover, or one side of the room may get all of the food.

Receptions can be tailored to any budget. Unlike other meal functions, you have more flexibility. There are many opportunities to be extravagant or frugal. For example, you can control the time allocated for the reception; you can offer a seafood bar with a few shrimp and a lot of inexpensive mussels arranged on crushed ice; or you can start with expensive hors d'oeuvres and back them up with cheese and dry snacks.

Generally speaking, if planners are paying per person, they would opt for buffet tables, dinner-sized plates, and self-service. On the other extreme, passed foods are appropriate if you are paying by consumption.

CHAPTER 10

Association and Corporate Events: The Business Side of Tourism

The Nuances of Working with Corporate Meeting Planners

Working with corporate planners in catering and conventions services can be an exercise in patience and humility. It also comes with many rewards and accolades!

Corporate planners, especially professional *third-party*[1] meeting planners working for the corporate planner, can be among the most organized and detailed. They can also be the most demanding and high maintenance.

This might be because they work with many "C" level executives. This creates a trickle-down response system.

If the meeting planner makes the "C" level team happy and you make the meeting planner happy, this results in great level of overall group satisfaction. Also known as a "Win-Win."

Achieving this can be extremely difficult due to the amount of variables. Among these can be monitoring the contracted suites versus the number of requested suites for each executive including the floor they are on, which tower they are in, the view, the room size and amenities, and so on.

It is important that the meeting planner identifies this to you as quickly as possible and it is communicated to the rooms' coordinator and in the group resume. These type of requests can be as simple as foam

---

[1] Third-party planners are hired by corporations and associations, to produce their meetings for them, instead of having an in-house planner.

pillows (*as opposed to feather*), to stocking the room with super premium vodka or as complex as ordering a particular name brand of treadmill and weights to be set in their suites. Having Starbucks coffee pods instead of the hotel standard is another example.

Catering for the corporate planner can be super fun when the budget is not the primary focus. In other words, their focus may be entertaining planners for future business and retention of loyal planners, rewarding top sales employees with *wow* events to retain great employees, overall creating events that guests will talk and reminisce about for years to come.

Many corporations have a reputation and a corporate culture to uphold. They need to project this with their internal staff as well as external planners, meaning they spend the necessary funds to sustain the best staff and entertain and attract the best planners. Therefore, menus for these planners are often themed multicourses and include signature drinks and wine pairings. Also these types of events combine live entertainment, celebrity acts, social media, and considerable audio-visual techniques and production.

On the menu planning side, this translates to offerings of an amuse bouche starter, a first course of soup and salad versus soup or salad, filet mignon instead of the current budget-conscious short rib, a dessert trio of custom delectables, including a corporate logo sugar piece, instead of a plain selection like an ordinary cheesecake.

On the convention service side, the corporate events can be extremely complex. These can include contracted concessions that can comprise some of the following:

- One complimentary room for every 40 booked rooms, on a cumulative basis
- Complimentary suites
- Complimentary suite upgrades
- Complimentary room amenities
- Waived charges for third and fourth person in a guestroom
- Rebate to master account as a booking incentive
- Discounts on food and beverage
- Discounts on audio-visual services when selecting the in-house provider

- Reduced resort fee
- Waived bartender fees
- Complimentary parking
- Discounted or complimentary staff and crew meals
- Contract date signing bonus, especially at a quarter's end

Corporate Meetings

Corporate meeting planners are more reliant on the CCSM as their *go to* person for everything! A CCSM is practically viewed as an extension of onsite planning team. Often this means the CCSMs are given a radio or telephone and are required to respond to all room setup, food, beverage, temperature control, and emergency needs as they arise.

In response to these regularly requested items, some hotels have provided a cell phone, tablet, or computer app that allows planners to request items such as:

- Extra chairs for a busy general session or breakouts
- Add heat or cooler air for a meeting room
- Refill water stations
- Request a food and beverage event be earlier or later
- Add easels, trashcans, pens and pads, and so on

While it is known that corporate meeting planners keep a CCSM very busy on the floor, they also are known to hire third-party planners.

On occasion the corporate planner may be an executive administrative assistant that is planning a small meeting and will not know much about any of the above-described items. In this case the CCSM must play the role of educator and assist in their future success.

This is an important role that can be sometimes overlooked by the novice CCSM. Often it feels like a burden to the CCSM, but is so valuable to both parties with an ending result of appreciation and loyalty. Remember, if the "C" levels are happy the event is a success!

Lastly, and much to the surprise and delight of CCSMs, corporate meeting planners are often generous with cash gratuities or gifts to the hotel operations teams.

Awards and Recognition Banquets

Many multiday meetings reserve one night to present awards. Meeting planners and CCSMs need to find ways to take the boredom out of awards presentations without sacrificing the recognition that winners deserve.

An awards banquet is often part of a grand banquet given on the last night of the meeting. However, this approach has several drawbacks. For one thing, guests have just survived an intense few days of meetings and other business activities and are ready to party. Most of them have probably been to one or more receptions earlier in the evening and have consumed a few alcoholic beverages. And if wine is served with the meal, the group may become loud. It is a shame that those who are *feeling good* continue the party while the awards are being presented. You really can't blame them if you have provided the liquor that is causing them to act in this way. They become oblivious to what is going on around them.

So, there is a new trend in the industry to present awards earlier in the meeting, such as on the first day. This ensures rapt attention from guests. It also allows the recipients to bask in the limelight throughout the rest of the meeting.

Also, many guests leave during the last day, not staying for the final banquet to avoid an extra night of hotel costs.

Awards can also be given at breakfasts or luncheons. Guests are a bit more alert during these times. Then they can have the last night free to have fun and unwind.

If there are several awards to be given, another tactic is to spread the presentations throughout the meeting. You could begin with the minor awards and save the most important, prestigious one for the last night.

If your planner still prefers the traditional final-night awards banquet, they could stagger the presentations between courses instead of scheduling them at the end of the meal. Dinner meals tend to run overtime; if all awards are presented at the end, chances are the program will have to begin before or during dessert. Some guests may not be paying attention. Embarrassing conversation may continue throughout the program. And some guests may even leave.

The CCSM must also be aware of the protocols, seating arrangements, and other similar considerations associated with various ceremonies.

How Most Beverage Functions Are Sold

Like meal functions, beverage functions can be packaged, priced, and sold in many different ways. But before evaluating the various options available, the meeting planner must first decide whether the beverage function will be offered as a:

Cash bar: Sometimes referred to as a *no-host bar*. Guests buy their own drinks, usually purchasing tickets from a cashier to exchange with a bartender for a drink. At small functions, the bartender may collect and serve, eliminating the cost of a cashier. Cashiers are usually charged as extra labor. However, cashiers provide better control and speed up service. Plus the bartenders do not have to handle dirty money and then handle glassware. A CCSM must have a conversation with the planner on what type of cash bar is provided at their hotel, especially if it is a true "cash bar" and does NOT accept credit card and guest room charges.

Open bar: Sometimes referred to as a *host* bar or *hosted* bar. Guests do not pay for their drinks. The meeting planner, or a sponsor, takes care of paying for everything. Liquor consumption is higher because someone else is paying. A sponsor can be the convention or meeting itself, an exhibitor, an outside supplier, and so on.

Combination bar: A blend of the cash bar and the open bar. The meeting planner can host the first hour, after which the bar reverts to a cash bar. The typical combination is when the meeting planner pays for each guest's first two drinks, and the guests then pay for any subsequent drinks personally. The meeting planner normally provides each guest with two drink tickets. After that, the guests buy their own drinks. Combination methods provide free drinks to guests, but retain control over costs and potential liability for providing unlimited drinks. If the planner purchases a bunch of drink tickets from the cashier upfront, and the guests don't use them all, the hotel may not give credit for the unused ones. Hotels depend on selling more drink tickets (*and meal tickets*) than planners can use.

Limited consumption bar: The meeting planner establishes a maximum dollar amount that he or she is prepared to spend. When serving drinks, the bartender rings up the price of each one, and when the maximum is reached, the bar is shut down. Typically the bar stays open, but reverts to a cash bar. This is a type of combination bar; however, instead of using the number of drinks as the break point, you use a dollar amount.

Charge Per Bottle

This is a common option for open bars and poured wine service used for meal functions. The meeting planner pays for all of the opened liquor bottles. A physical inventory is taken at the beginning and end of the function to determine liquor usage. Most hotels charge for each opened bottle, even if only one drink was poured from it.

This pricing method saves money, but is inconvenient to monitor and calculate. You will not know the final cost until the event is over. Usually the group history will give some indication of how much consumption to expect. Opened bottles usually cannot be removed from the property.

You can have opened and unopened bottles delivered to a hospitality suite, to the room of a VIP to use during the convention or meeting, or to another beverage function scheduled later on. In the case of wine, you can try to use it for a meal function later on, or you might include it in complimentary fruit baskets for meeting VIPs.

Note: Wine lists provided on catering menus are priced by the bottle. This is for higher end wines, not offered on the bar.

Charge Per Drink

This is a common option for a cash bar. This method uses drink tickets or a cash register for control. Normally, the price per drink is high enough to cover all expenses in addition to the cost of the liquor (*e.g., garnishes, cocktail napkins, drink stirrers, etc.*).

Individual drink prices are set to yield a standard beverage cost percentage established by the caterer. The hotel's cost percentages range from about 12 to 18 percent for spirits and usually around 25 percent for beer and wine.

If the meeting planner is picking up the drink tab, he or she will not know the final cost until the event is over. However, if the guests are paying for their own drinks, this is irrelevant.

Charge Per Person

This is a common option for open bars. Food is usually included. This method is more expensive for the meeting planner, but less work and hassle for them. They choose a plan, such as premium liquors for 1 hour, and then tell the CCSM how many people are coming. Costs are known ahead of time—no surprises. If, for instance, you have 500 guests and the charge is $25.00 apiece, you know that the total charge will be $12,500.00 plus tax, plus gratuity, and can budget accordingly and confidently.

Tickets are usually collected from guests at the door, and the guarantee is monitored and enforced. The meeting planner must provide a firm guarantee before negotiating a per-person charge. Often a banquet server will count guests at the door using a clicker.

Charge Per Hour

This option is similar to the charge per person. In fact, it is common for CCSMs to include a version of the per-person pricing method when pricing this option. This option often includes a sliding scale, with higher cost for the first hour. This is because guests usually eat and drink more during the first hour, then level off.

Here's a typical example of how this option is priced: there is a $25.00 per-person charge for the first hour, and a $20.00 per person charge for the second hour. If the function has, say, 100 guests for a 2-hour reception, the total charge would be $4,500.00 [($25.00 × 100) + ($20.00 × 100)] plus, plus.[2]

Like the per-person option, the meeting planner must provide a firm guarantee before negotiating a per-hour charge. And the guarantee is monitored and enforced. Furthermore, no consideration is given for those who arrive late or leave early; in the example above, the charge is $45.00 per person, regardless.

---

[2] Plus, plus (often abbreviated as ++) means plus tax, plus gratuity. These are fees that are added to the price of the meal.

Flat-Rate Charge

This option is similar to the price per person and to the price per hour.

The meeting planner pays a flat rate for the function. Typically, the CCSM will assume that each guest will drink about two drinks per hour for the first hour and one drink per hour thereafter. If your group does not drink this much, you may be able to negotiate a lower price.

The total charge will vary based on the number of guests; whether well, call, or premium brands are poured; how many unique products the caterer must provide; type of service; and the type of food served.

This is an easy way to purchase a beverage function. No matter how many drinks guests consume, or how much food they eat, the meeting planner will know in advance what the total cost will be. They will not have to worry about exceeding their budget. Nor will they have to wait for an inventory of opened liquor containers or an audit of the number of drinks prepared and served. There are no unwelcome surprises.

The Best Option?

This depends on so many variables that it is difficult to generalize. We can conclude, though, that the typical hotel tends to earn more sales revenue and more profit with the per-person option. Consider the following example, using typical beverage charges:

The hotel charges $80.00 for a bottle of bourbon that yields 27¼ ounce drinks. Each drink, therefore, costs the meeting planner $2.96. If guests are expected to drink two drinks per hour, a 1-hour reception for 1,000 guests would cost almost $6,000.00 plus, plus if the planner purchased the event on a per-bottle basis.

If the planner purchased the event on a per drink basis, the cost per drink would be higher; let's say it would be $6.00 per drink. In that case, the event would cost the same group $12,000.00 plus, plus.

If they purchase the event for a cost per person, the price charged by the hotel would typically be over twice the normal cost per drink; let's say it would be $20.00 per person, all-you-can-drink (*no food*). In that case, the event would cost the group $20,000.00 plus, plus.

The hotel usually earns more with the per-person option, which is why CCSMs like to push that option more than the others.

The per-person option, though, may be economical in some cases. For instance, since the average consumption in a 1-hour reception is two or more drinks per-person, if the cost for, say, two-and-a-half drinks calculated under the per-drink charge exceeds the cost per person option, the planner should take the per-person option. They won't see this discrepancy very often, but if they do, they should take advantage of it.

The per-person option may also be better than the per-bottle choice for the planner. In the examples above, the per-bottle choice seems pretty good. However, the potential total cost of $6,000.00 plus, plus may be seriously underestimated. For instance, if there are no pouring controls in place, there can be a lot of over pouring and spillage, which the planner will end up paying for.

Note: Per drink, per person charges include standard mixers and garnishes with the drink price. Per bottle charges do not include these.

Receptions: Setup and Other Considerations

Receptions are sometimes referred to as *walk and talks*, and are often predinner functions that are designed primarily to encourage guests to get to know one another. Most meetings schedule an opening reception as an *ice-breaker* to allow guests to make new friends and renew old acquaintances. If an opening reception is not scheduled, a guest will possibly only meet the handful of people sitting at his or her dining table.

When planning a reception, it is best to locate several food buffet stations around the room. Each station should offer a different type of food. This will encourage guests to move around the room and socialize. If possible, you should include one or two action stations. You also should have a server at each station to replenish foods, bus soiled tableware, remove trash, and be a psychological deterrent to curb people's tendencies to heap their plates or return several times.

The amount of food consumed may also depend on how many square feet are available for guests to move around in. Plan for 5½ to 10 square feet of floor space per guest. Tighter space equals less consumption. With 5½ to 6 square feet, people will feel a bit tight and have more difficulty getting to the food and beverage stations—they may eat and drink less.

Seating should be minimized at receptions. You do not want to encourage guests to sit and eat; remember, you want to promote mingling and networking. Seating should be provided for no more than 25 to 30 percent of the count. Cabaret-style seating, highboy tables, or park benches, with little or no table space, are suitable.

If a cost-conscious meeting planner is paying a low-price per person where guests can eat and drink as much as they want, the CCSM will typically allocate about 6 square feet per person to keep the price low and the food and beverage costs under control.

Note: When helping a planner order food for a reception, it is important to know a few tips:

- Shrimp and sushi are among the most popular items and guests typically will put five or six on their plate (*use small plates*).
- Cheese displays and pasta stations last longer than most other food offerings.

An area of 10 square feet provides ample space for guests to mingle and visit the food and beverage stations easily. It is an appropriate amount of floor space for a luxury-type reception.

Table placement at receptions affects food consumption. An hors d'oeuvre table placed against a wall provides only 180-degree access to the food. A rectangular table in the center of the room provides two open sides and 360-degree access to the food. A round table in the center of the room gives an appearance of a lavish presentation, but there is no way for a line to form to circle the table. Guests have to work their way in and out at various points for each item they wish to eat, which decreases food consumption. The round table in this case is sometimes referred to as a Rubik's Cube, because of guest frustration at trying to get to the food.

Food stations need enough floor space for the tables and aisles. An 8-foot long rectangular banquet table needs about 24 square feet for the table, and about 60 square feet for aisle space if the table is against the wall. About 100 square feet for aisle space is needed if the table is accessible from all sides.

One of the biggest complaints at opening receptions is that the music is too loud. Many people haven't seen each other for a year and want to talk, and there are generally a lot of introductions going on. Usually the reception is a networking event, and guests end up having to shout over the music to be heard. If loud music is desired, wait until later in the evening, or for the final night banquet.

A three-piece jazz combo is a nice live background music offering for receptions.

Bars and neutral beverage stations should be spaced around the room. Bars should be placed sufficient distances from the food stations so that people have to change locations in order to get a drink. This further increases mingling.

- When setting up portable bars for a very large function, you can reduce space estimates by having them located in pairs. Leave the space in front of the bars clean and clear of anything, so as to allow lines to form.
- Place two or four portable bars back-to-back in the middle of the room so the bars can share a common area for glassware, ice, wines, beers, and so on. Eliminates duplicate storage areas and free up extra floor space.
- Self-service, nonalcoholic beverage stations, the setups are similar to buffet-table setups.
- A hot-beverage station will need as much space as a buffet table.
- Tended bars will need more floor space because you need room to store back-up stock, ice, and coolers to hold beer and some wines.
- Allocate enough working space for bartenders and any cocktail servers.
- The smallest portable bar measures approximately 6 feet by 7 feet, or about 42 square feet.
- Consider aisle and other space needed, you will need to allocate at least 150 square feet for the typical portable banquet-bar setup.

CHAPTER 11

Casino, VIP and Celebrity Events, and Tradeshows: Dealing with the Rich and Famous

Casino Events

Casino events are different than any other type of catering event because of the guest profile. Casino events are usually high end for the food, beverage, décor, and entertainment. These events can range from plated duet dinners with lavish first courses of seafood and theme desserts and signature drinks for events such as New Year's Eve (*perhaps, followed by a celebrity concert*), to brunches for daytime-themed slot tournaments, to indoor-outdoor reception-style-themed buffets for events such as July 4 celebrations.

However, casino events are typically shorter in length—often an hour to an hour and a half, compared to most celebratory events of three to four hours for convention final-night galas, nonprofit and social events. The reason casino events are designed to be shorter in length is to have the guest back on the casino floor gaming as much as possible for the duration of their stay.

The success of these events is measured by the amount of gaming tracked on the guests' loyalty cards and the returned survey scores and comments.

In a casino hotel, casino marketing controls all comps. They can take a booked meeting room away with just a few hours' notice for a high roller event.

CCSMs have to be able to pull an event off for high rollers with very little notice.

Working in Casinos Environments and with Casino Marketing Events

This is a whole world unto itself. For some, it is a mystery that a casino property spends so much money and resources on elaborate events and for some of us it's a way of doing in-house events with huge and immediate financial returns. While these events may cost over a million dollars to produce with marketing, entertainment, food and beverage, the return in gaming revenues while the guests are on property is instantaneous. Loyalty gaming cards and the database that tracks play are vital to the analytics of casino. These cards, used in slot machines, can track the amount of money played, the duration of time played and other player behaviors. For player guests who game at the tables, such as blackjack, craps, and roulette, the loyalty card information must be manually entered by a *pit boss*.

The participants have in the past been stereotypically called *high rollers* or *whales*. Today, they are known by their level of loyalty card ranking. Each ranked player has a property-specific theoretical worth in points and is categorized and tracked as such. These events are designed to bring high-rated casino players for a promotional *casino paid* event which in-turn actually brings them to game on the casino floor before and after the sponsored event. People often ask if it is the amount a guest loses gaming that determines how high they are rated. While that helps, it might be more about how much the guest takes chances to keep playing for longer periods of time and repeats the cycle of winning and giving back, and so on.

Some casino marketing events are slot tournaments that are sponsored or sometimes require a guest to *buy in* and have an advertised prize payout that is usually on a sliding scale divided up by the top 10 or 20 scores.

CCSMs that are fortunate enough to gain experience in casino marketing and special events will often be exposed to creating lavish events. Events of this nature have themes with lavish over-the-top room décor, floral displays, and food and beverage offerings. In addition to the afore-mentioned slot tournaments, these can include annual events such as:

- New Year's Eve dinners, concerts, and fireworks
- New Year's Day brunches

- Super Bowl (*legally called "the Big Game"*) viewing parties with tailgating-type food and satellite wagering outside the ballroom
- March Madness college basketball events
- July 4 parties
- Multiple shopping events where players can spend their loyalty points, especially over the holidays

For a CCSM, these events are super fun to be around, watching guests enjoying themselves in elegant surroundings. For those CCSMs with a love of catering, these events often provide a once-in-a-lifetime opportunity to create themed menus for an audience who is likely to appreciate them. Consider ideas such as a reception of hors d'oeuvres of gazpacho shooters, a Caesar salad served from a martini shaker, a Tomahawk steak carving station, a house-made Yukon gold, sweet and Peruvian purple potato chip station, a gelato and candy station, and festive layered signature drink beverage bars.

Because the casinos are geared for adult-only entertainment, working in this environment requires specific training in recognizing possible underage gambling and drinking, child endangerment, and problem gambling.

Conventions service in casinos alters your job slightly from traditional (*nongaming*) hotels and facilities. Highly rated or VIP casino players and guests will often have precedence over a convention meeting planner and their VIPs. These can be manifested in preferential parking, hotel check-in, assigned suites, restaurant reservations, and so on.

However, the meeting and convention offerings at many casino or hotel properties have more leisure time attractions than most other (*nongaming*) hotels or resorts. These common influencers can include:

- Casino gaming
- Complimentary beverages for gaming guests
- Complimentary entertainment
- Celebrity shows and concerts
- Nightclubs off the hotel or casino lobby
- A plethora of restaurants and often celebrity restaurants

- Attached high-end shopping centers
- Resort and outdoor activities, including gaming at pools
- 24 × 7 operations

The cons of working in a catering and convention services in the casino environment may include:

- Walking through casinos that allow cigarette smoking
- Working around intoxicated guests
- Sometimes parking a long distance from your office

Nonetheless, the pros heavily outweigh the cons, including:

- Working in some of the world's largest hotels
- 24 hours of employee-free meals
- Planners have easy access to cash, resulting in more frequent and more generous tipping
- Meeting people from all over the world
- Being part of a team of CCSMs—these teams often work together on events
- Working and learning from the best in the business, your peers and supervisors

Entertainment Riders

The recent report that Beyoncé's Super Bowl rider[1] was leaked brings to mind that riders are something CCSMs and planners should pay attention to.

Riders are amendments to entertainment contracts. They set the specifications and requests of the entertainers. They fall into two categories: hospitality and technical.

---

[1] www.cnn.com/video/#/video/showbiz/2013/01/31/sbt-beyonce-super-bowl-rider.hln

Hospitality can include specific food and beverages, towels, transportation, hotels, a runner for personal shopping, comp tickets for their entourage, security, locking of rooms, ice, and so on.

When celebrities are hired to perform at your hotel they typically are contracted with their standard "riders." These riders can be very complicated and out of the norm for what your property usually has in inventory.

These often require items that a person would have in their private home such as:

- A dressing room that is more like a living room with floor lamps, table lamps, couches, love seats, tables, chairs, bath towels (*both black and white*), hand towels, facial tissue, coat racks, telephones, fax machines, hard line, and complimentary Wi-Fi.
- Specialty food and beverage items, such as:
  o Raw and organic foods
  o Vegan food, soy products, steamed vegetables, lean chicken with no butter or oil or spices, jars of honey, green tea
  o Premade items such as hardboiled eggs, peanut butter and jelly sandwiches, deli platters with cold cooked meats such as salmon and chicken and beef, white bread with the crusts cut off
  o Specific candies, such as a particular flavor of jelly beans, M&M candies, and chewing gum
  o High-end and often international gourmet and hard-to-find soft drinks, energy drinks and waters, often packaged in awkward-sized bottles, containers, and so on
  o High-end bottles of wines and beer, and spirits with bottle openers, specified number of glasses that don't often match and exceed the number of entertainers in the room
- Room atmospheric items such as specific types of floral and color of black-out curtains, candles, types of drinking straws, air purifiers and space heaters
- CCSMs available 24 × 7, but staff not allowed to speak to the celebrities they are serving

Additionally, celebrities often arrive with an entourage of people which can include agents, managers, back-up singers, choreographers, dancers and more dancers, tons of production crew members, handlers, make-up artist, hair dressers, chefs, massage therapists, seamstresses, personal assistants, security personnel, spouses, significant others, and children. It is the celebrity entourage that will often cause more issues and stress than the celebrities themselves.

Technical riders can include requests or demands for specific types of pianos, sound system specifications, lighting requirements, size and position of a riser, how many and types of local crew members that are needed, and so on.

Some riders have been considered unreasonable, until the reason is explained. For example, a request for all white furniture may be to insure that the furniture is clean and sanitary.

Paul McCartney requested a sweep of the venue by bomb sniffing dogs before the show.

Some riders are notorious, such as Van Halen's 1982 rider with a request for no brown M&Ms.[2] Their rider was 53 pages long, and by checking to see if there were any brown M&Ms, they could tell if the rider had been read thoroughly. It was a signal for them to check to see if other things in the rider had been missed.

It is important to read the riders thoroughly. There are most likely expenses in there that you need to know about in advance. Riders can be negotiated. Some of the requirements may only apply to concert halls and stadiums, and must be adapted to hotel function rooms. This may include extra security, backstage passes, feeding of an entourage, and so on.

Head Table Seating Protocol

Protocol is defined as rules of etiquette and ceremony.

The planner should develop the protocol for order of rank. This will depend on your organization. A corporation may list the CEO as number one, whereas an association may list the volunteer chairman of the board rather than the paid association executive.

---

[2] http://tywkiwdbi.blogspot.com/2011/08/why-van-halen-demanded-no-brown-m.html

If someone is offering an invocation (*where appropriate*), he or she may be seated at the head table. All seats at the head table should be filled, and it is usual to seat those who have a role in the program during that session.

If it is an awards dinner, the honorees should be given high priority. If there is a noted speaker, he or she should also be high on the list.

The event host or hostess should be seated in the center of the table, with the main VIP seated to his or her right. The second most important person should be seated to the left of the host or hostess. It then continues right, left, right, left, until the table is filled.

If there is a lectern on the table, the host or hostess would be seated to the right of the lectern, and seating would again go right, left, right, left.

Everyone at the head table should be formally introduced at the beginning of the meeting or event.

Additional head tables may be arranged to seat all those who need to be seated at the head table. There have been head tables for 48 chefs at a culinary convention. There were 4 rows of 12, with each back row elevated in tiers on risers. (*It was difficult to follow protocol for this event, because many of the chefs were the size of the late chef, Paul Prudhomme, who was one of the chefs at the table. This meant they had to take the weight of the chefs into consideration so the weight would be evenly distributed.*) In the case of tiered tables, the first, or closest table to the audience would be for the highest ranking officials and guests.

Each seat at the head table should have a place card, thus eliminating confusion on who sits where.

The head table should always be served first.

It is important to have a responsible member of your staff remain in charge of the head table arrangements to give special consideration to details and to foresee problems before they occur.

Sports Events

Sports and special event planners typically work in domestic and international areas that host annual events with major televised media. These planners generally plan and travel at the whims of the crew, meaning media technicians and staff. However, they require budget catering or provide their own catering crews on a budget. Working with these planners can often be filled with last-minute and ever-changing requests. This is a very fluid industry!

Celebrity Chefs

Some planners want their gala done by a celebrity chef. You would have to have extremely deep pockets to actually make this happen. They are rarely even at their own restaurants. They are too busy making television shows or traveling to food events.

And, there is a hierarchy in *chefdom*. Chefs that cook food to-order have said that food is at its best when freshly prepared, one dish at a time. They disdain the celebrity chef contestants on the television competition shows that come from the catering world—where food is prepared in batches and held for a time before serving. But banquet chefs do much better in some of the challenges, because they are faster and used to high-volume cooking.

Most celebrity chefs come from the *cook to order* world. Very few celebrity chefs do catering. An exception is Wolfgang Puck, who has a catering division. However, you won't see him at the events, unless it is high visibility event, like the Oscars.

Obviously, a celebrity chef with multiple restaurants around the globe cannot be at every restaurant. So they have *shadow chefs*. A shadow chef is a chef that cooks items from another chef's menu, instead of creating their own menu items.

In a restaurant, chefs are pretty much doing everything. Depending on the size of the restaurant, they may have a sous chef (*under chef, #2 in the kitchen*) or a prep cook (*that cleans and cuts vegetables, measure out ingredients, etc.*).

Hotels have all kinds of specialized chefs. In Las Vegas, where buffets rule, there are buffet chefs. And, there are banquet chefs.

Other chef specialty areas are listed in Chapter 6.

Exhibits and Tradeshows

Being part of this mega-million-dollar industry of tradeshows is amazing!

As a CCSM you may get the opportunity to manage tradeshows of many sizes. This can include a few tabletop exhibits that small meetings will host in your meeting rooms or foyers to the world's largest annual tradeshows held in convention center facilities, such as CES (*Consumer Electronics Show*).

Some of these shows are meant for a select audience and some for a mass consumer or public market. These events represent revenue generation opportunities for planners and, in fact, may be their only source of income for the entire year.

For guests and consumers, tradeshows present a first-hand look at a company's latest and greatest offerings, inventions, and product launches. This can include anything and everything, including places to travel to, lifesaving equipment or drugs, pet supplies, education at all levels, homeowners projects, veterans' health care and cyber security, to highlight a few.

Most breakfasts, lunches, and receptions held in the tradeshow areas will be arranged with the meeting planners, while the individual booth orders will be organized directly with the exhibitor.

For CCSMs in hotels, tradeshows can present a ton of food and beverage opportunities with the exhibitors directly. Caution should be had here not to overcommit your operations team running around chasing custom booth orders. An easier and more controllable means of servicing tradeshow booths are with limited menus. These can include a la carte energy bars, pastries, beverages and bars, savory snacks, and candy.

For CCSMs in facilities and primarily in convention centers, these types of limited menus are probably the standard offerings. Booths within a convention center can range from the standard 10 feet × 10 feet, 10 feet × 20 feet to large prefabricated offices of 90 feet × 100 feet and more.

There is one particular type of tradeshow that can impact the facilities operations more than others. These are the food tradeshows. At these types of shows almost all exhibitors will have needs ranging from ice, use of your kitchen, rental of cooking, and serving equipment to housing of large refrigeration units placed at the loading dock. Many of these will be limited to a 2-ounce sampling size of service to full service menu items with dedicated banquet service staff. Often a CCSM or banquet staff will be stationed on the tradeshow floor taking care of ice and equipment orders.

As a CCSM you will again be working with preferred vendors and external tradeshow planners that travel with planners.

Full-service, top-of-the-line convention exhibit companies such as The Freeman Company[3] can provide the following services:

- Traditional booth setup of tables, chairs, wastebasket, pipe-and-drape backdrop and coordinated daily or nightly booth cleaning services
- Exhibit and tradeshow booth, aisle signage and exhibitor branding
- Registration counters, usually freestanding in foyers and meeting rooms
- Digital branding and manufactured signage—interactive and static directional, schedule of events, meeting announcement, sponsor thank you signs, and so on
- Convention and general session entry units
- Electrical service coordination to individual exhibitor booths
- Audio-visual, IT services and technologies, including convention apps
- Full general session event production

Exhibit companies really create an overall branded experience for the guests through visual and audio media with the latest in IT technologies.

CCSMs, along with their operations departments, will need to monitor the load-in and load-out process of these companies. A walk-through with the exhibit company representative and the hotel staff of the areas used to house the tradeshow or exhibit area prior to load-in, when the room is clean and clear of anything is a must. This is a similar experience to when you rent a car and are asked to check or confirm of any dings, dents, or damage prior to driving off the rental lot. This process will need to be repeated again following the load-out. It is at this time any damages to doors, walls, carpet, flooring, elevators, and so on will be documented, signed off by both parties and repair estimates later sent to the exhibit company.

---

[3] *www.freemanco.com*

Tradeshows are a *turn and burn* part of our business. A tradeshow loads-in for a couple of days, is full of guests for the next couple of days, spends another couple of days to load out, and then it all starts over again. Heavy forklift equipment with pallets delivered to booths swiftly running through your ballrooms and facilities can take a toll on the soft goods and infrastructure. Keep up with a best practices procedure on monitoring and reporting maintenance items to your director or operations departments.

Additional items to plan for when working tradeshows and exhibitors are:

- Confirm and compare with the planner and the tradeshow provider on times for load-in, load-out, exhibitor load-in, actual tradeshow hours for each day, timing of meal events
- Have planner approve locations of group food and beverage service such as buffets and bars
- Verify exhibitor and vendor meals, if any
- Prepare for loading out of exhibitors that do not ship items through exhibit companies

CCSMs need to be aware of the importance of the exhibitor to the planner. Planners providing tradeshows rely on the revenues generated by booth rentals and year-over-year repeat exhibitors. You can do your part to help the overall great guest experience of the exhibitor, in turn helping the planner achieve repeat business for their tradeshow and the trickle-down effect of repeat business to your company. This can be as simple walking the tradeshow floor before opening and greeting exhibitors and engaging in conversation to check their satisfaction with your hotel and facilities.

CHAPTER 12

Upselling for Repeat Business and Working with Vendors: Improving the Bottom Line

Upsell is a common term in the hospitality industry, referring to the increase in the amount a planner spends above what their contracted minimum or what their initial order was. Sometimes a planner doesn't know what they're missing until you point out to them what they can have. The CCSM must present this in a way that is affordable or a slight stretch to their budget, but so worth it.

A CCSM must tell the story by painting a picture in the planner's mind of how much better their event will be received by guests, sponsors, and their leadership if just a few key items are added. It must be practical, impressionable, and delightful. For example, the simple addition of some LED uplighting in a room is dramatic. Other examples include: electronic signage for bars, dinner menus, and sponsor recognition. A champagne welcome toast (*by CEO or sponsor*) at a dinner function is so classy and unexpected, and a trio dessert with a chocolate logo is such a happy ending! All of the above are easy upsells that can elevate an event from ordinary to extraordinary, with equivalent funds that planners would spend on items of lesser impact and greater environmental waste such as name tags, menu cards, and programs.

There are just four ways to grow your business:

1. Increase the number of planners.
2. Increase the frequency with which they deal with you.
3. Increase the average value of the sales transaction.

4. Improve the effectiveness of the processes in your meeting, hotel, and so on.

Upselling is addressing the third way, increasing the value of the sales transaction. Fast food is an example when they ask, "*Do you want fries with that?*"

If you and your staff aren't trained on effective ways to upsell, chances are you either offend potential planners by being too pushy or leave money on the table that planners would have willingly spent with you. Either option is costly.

Upselling is when you help a planner decide to buy a little extra or upgrade the final purchase slightly. The bonus is that upselling can be extremely profitable for you as the sales person and for your facility.

Upselling usually takes place after the initial sale has been made. At this point, upselling should be easy:

- The major purchase has been made.
- Rapport has already been established.
- You have identified their needs.
- You have presented benefits.
- You have handled objections.
- Upselling, then, is just "*by the way.*"

The three biggest mistakes in upselling:

- No attempt is made to upsell.
- The salesperson comes across as being pushy.
- The upselling pitch is made in an unconvincing manner so the planner generally refuses.

The wrong way to upsell:

- You are at a restaurant and just finished a big meal.
- The server asks, "*Would you care for dessert?*"
- If you say "*Yes,*" you might give the impression of overindulging, so many customers refuse out of habit. Result—no sale.

The right way to upsell:

- The savvy server doesn't ask if the member wants dessert.
- The professional *assumes* that when people go out for a meal they are treating themselves.
- Of course they'll want to treat themselves to dessert.
- In this case, the server pulls up the dessert tray and says: *"To finish off your meal with a little something sweet* (that's the benefit) *I brought the dessert tray over for you. Would you like to hear about the most popular ones?"* (Asks permission to proceed.)
- When the planner agrees to hear about the desserts the server doesn't just list them by name; he describes their benefits. Instead of saying, *"This is chocolate mousse,"* he'd say something like, *"If you like chocolate you'll love this. We've got a chocolate mousse that melts in your mouth."*

Profits come when you get the planner to purchase:

- Additional items
- Bigger items
- Better items
- More expensive items
- Additional services

Don't get greedy:

- Upgrade *slightly*
- Do not be pushy
- Know the value of your products
- Develop new options

For CCSMs, catering is more than just selling food! It is about creating a special experience by coordinating food and beverage with décor, ambiance, presentation, service-style, and entertainment. Each area is an upsell opportunity.

Upselling is part consultation and part selling. It should focus on increasing the average check, but also on enhancing guest satisfaction. It is a subtle, but important difference. Sales staff must understand the planner and recognize their expectations, so that appropriate recommendations can be made. Assess the planner: if you get a frown when you initiate suggestive selling, stop immediately.

Try to make the planner feel special.

There are a number of ways for a caterer to increase revenue:

- Better marketing mix (*more corporate events, fewer coffee receptions*)
- Selling more beverages
- Charging room rental
- Raising prices
- Adding off-premise catering
- Higher check average (*which is upselling*)

Sales managers need training. For example: Instead of asking, "*Do you want to serve wine?*" Ask, "*Do you prefer a red or a white wine?*"

When you are upselling, you must assume the planner will naturally want this. Begin with a brief benefit. Add something unique. Ask for permission to describe it.

- Convince the planner to upgrade the menu and spend more money.
- It is suggesting or recommending specific "*extras.*"
- It could be changing the main course from chicken to beef filet, adding a duet or trio specialty dessert, or serving a better quality wine.
- Space upsells could include room rental, charges for specific room sets, or rooms with views.

For a CCSM, food is the easiest thing to upsell. Examples would be passed hors d' oeuvres or regional specialties (*Salmon in Seattle or Crab Cakes in Baltimore, etc.*). Most areas have specialties that they are known for. Being in the middle of the desert, in Las Vegas we specialize in the buffet.

Menu Upgrades:

- Upgrade cut or quality of meat
- Champagne toasts
- Theme bars (*Martini, Margarita*)
- Specialty theme drinks
- Fancy garnishes
- Caesar salad (*made tableside*)

Additional courses that can be upsold:

- Intermezzo
- Cheese cart
- Cordial service
- Fancier hors d 'oeuvres
- Hot hors d' oeuvres
- Petit fours
- Ice carvings
- Station enhancements

Continental upsells:

- Freshly baked breads and pastries
- Gourmet coffee (*flavored, cappuccino, latte, etc.*)
- Breakfast sandwich (*croissant with egg, ham, cheese or a breakfast burrito*)

Upsells for the health conscious planner:

- Organic foods
- Low fat recipes
- Low carb offerings
- Sugar-free options
- Fresh anything
- No transfats
- No HFCS (*High Fructose Corn Syrup*)

Other:

- Place card calligraphy
- Upgraded china
- Candelabras
- Linen overlays or table runners
- Chair covers
- Ceiling swags
- Disposables (*imprinted napkins, cups, etc.*)
- Customized tabletop settings
- Plants and foliage
- Table favors
- Extra staff
- French or Russian service

Afterglow

There is no better way to end the dinner portion of an event than to schedule an afterglow. And, it is a great upsell. Dinner is over—it's time for coffee and dessert. People are full, yet the planner wants the guests to interact, dance, and have a good time. Rather than force-feed them a calorie-laden dessert, let them get up and move about a bit before tackling the sweets.

- Afterglow stations are a great way to do this. Serve the following at stations around the room: cappuccino, espresso, international coffees, cognacs, cordials, and bite size signature desserts.
- An afterglow can also be held in a separate room, away from the room where the dinner was held. An afterglow would be most likely be preferred by those who want to get away from loud music and have a place to talk. They can enjoy coffees and desserts at their own pace. If the budget allows, the planner can add cordials.
- Put in some lounge furniture like easy chairs, sofas, and coffee tables to make it comfortable and inviting.

- An afterglow can also be a brunch event following a previous night's wedding reception.
- *International coffee TO GO station*: This station features a few types of flavored coffees with chocolate shavings, whipped cream, cinnamon, cane sugar sticks, flavored syrups, and of course coffee cups to go! Paper cups are easier to mix and mingle with than cups and saucers.
- If there is a sponsor for the dinner, the planner can seek a separate sponsor for the afterglow.

There are many reasons to approach upselling for events. Among these are:

- Getting planners to meet their food and beverage minimums
- Getting planners to exceed their food and beverage minimums
- Improving a CCSM's incentives
- Increasing house profits that lead to additional resources for bonus and FF&E[1]
- Increasing the average check amount for certain events to benefit all stakeholders
- Increasing the overall worth on a planner's business for future bookings and forecasting

In the past, CCSMs focused mainly on food and beverage items such as table wine service, intermezzo, and coffee-to-go stations (*which are all still excellent upsells*), but the playing field has now increased with so many more opportunities. Among these are:

- Celebrity chef inspired hors d'oeuvres, entrees, and dessert offerings
- Fruit, vegetable, and herb-infused waters at breaks and meals

---

[1] FF&E: Furniture, Fixtures, and Equipment.

- High protein additions to meal such as hard boiled eggs, raw organic nuts, and nut butters included or instead of dips with crudités, Greek yogurt versus traditional yogurts, adding tuna and egg salads to deli buffets
- Stations of super food for receptions like: everything avocado, assorted legumes, berries, and meat jerkies
- Four-course dinner menu (*with elegant service*) all the way to a 12-course chef's tasting menu (*need guests with plenty of time and a food mentality*)
- Beverage du Jour stations (*whatever is popular at the moment*), for instance Sangria, Moscow Mule, Prosecco, Manhattans, craft beers, and Tequila tastings; and for casino properties, anything with flair bartender stations and especially award-winning bartenders
- Wine pairing for each course (*be sure you have the stemware and room on the table for this*)
- Dessert stations, from molecular gastronomy offerings of fruit caviar and antigriddles to make-on-site frozen treats to build your own s'mores with iced coffee and latte *foodscapes*

By far the most profitable upsell for hotels are … *drum roll, please* … ROOM RENTAL FEES! At some facilities, CCSMs may even be incentivized solely on room rental as an *aftercontract* upsell opportunity. If the room rental includes food and beverage events, then room setup charges will probably cover the room setup labor. If quoting room rental for a meeting, a CCSM should quote a higher room rental to cover the labor cost as due diligence. The shorter term the event books, the higher the room rental you can charge. This is simple supply and demand economics. This is especially true for major convention cities hosting citywide convention groups.

Other standard upsell or marketing opportunities that include other departments of the hotel at most properties include the following:

- Custom room key card advertising anything from an event to a sponsor to a new product or logo or merger launch. These typically have a minimum order and require the hotel's upper-management approval.

- Custom branding throughout the hotel or conference center, ranging from signage to room drops to room service amenities.
- At some properties the CCSM will be able to upsell complete themes, such as in-house or outsourced décor, props, ice carvings, centerpieces, floral, linens, transportation, offsite venues, and for the casino properties entertainment, casino shows, restaurant reservations, flair bartenders, and so on. In other properties this can be totally outsourced to DMCs,[2] which in turn provides your property with commissions (*with the commission being your upsell*).

The key to effective upsell is *the picture*! This includes the ability to paint the picture (*in the planner's mind*) of guests enjoying the experience, sponsors enjoying the value of their contribution, and their leadership enjoying easy, professionalism, and how proud they are at that particular moment. A CCSM should follow this up with sending actual photographs of rooms sets, food and beverage stations and, whenever possible, other group experiences. Do this before the future planner asks, as a way to anticipate their needs.

Lastly, the best person to rebook the group is the CCSM who has just successfully executed a convention sales group with upsell of increased revenue for all stakeholders, all the while preserving customer satisfaction throughout the process, driving this process for future bookings and inviting the planner back at every turn is the ultimate extension of the sales team.

Hospitality Suites

Hospitality suites are places for guests to gather outside of the meeting. Hospitality suites can be hosted by the sponsoring organization, a chapter of the organization, an exhibitor, a nonexhibiting corporation, an allied association, or a person running for an office in the organization.

---

[2] DMC: Destination Management Company. Association for Destination Management Executives (ADME) www.adme.com.

Hospitality suites are considered ICW business (*in conjunction with*), meaning they piggyback on top of other meetings and conventions. Be sure you know how much is being spent on hospitality suites that are held by others during the event. They count as part of the value of the meeting when you are negotiating. Additionally, the revenue generated may count toward the food and beverage minimum spend.

Some planners retain right of approval on who can book suites at your hotel(s) during their meeting dates, to limit access to companies that may decide to hold a hospitality suite in lieu of exhibiting at their show.

They are normally open after dinner until late in the evening, often not starting until after 10:00 p.m. Occasionally, they may open up earlier in the day. Hospitality suites may offer a continental breakfast during the early part of the day, dry snacks, and soft drinks during the afternoon, and liquor and food during the evening.

Some suites offer a full bar, some beer, and wine only. Some have a plentiful variety of food, while others have only dry snacks. Some just offer a Viennese dessert table with specialty coffees and possibly liqueurs.

The host should consider ordering more food, and different types of foods, if the guests have had an open evening. Some of them may have skipped going to dinner on their own, and so may be quite hungry when they show up.

Hospitality suites are usually held in a suite on a sleeping room floor, and are often serviced by the hotel room service department, even if they are sold by catering. If they are held in a public function room they would be sold and serviced by the catering department.

An advantage to a public function room is that there is usually room for entertainment and guests can navigate more easily around a crowded room.

If you do use a function room for the hospitality suite, soften the feel of the sterile function room. Perhaps add some greenery or screens, something to soften the look. You may be able to get the planner to rent custom furniture from the companies that rent to tradeshow exhibitors. Don't forget background music.

But no matter what you do, the public areas will never look as nice as a hotel suite. The suite has that homey feel because of the living room furniture throughout. It may also offer a great view of the outside areas.

This is a type of business that restaurants and night-clubs can seek out if they are conveniently located in relation to a hotel or conference center. In Las Vegas, for example, many independent restaurants with private dining rooms are located right inside the hotels.

Regardless of the location, do not allow people to self-serve alcohol and do not leave any function you sponsor unattended by a staffer.

Be on the lookout for *underground hospitality suites* where unofficial parties pop up, with guests bringing in their own liquor. This is one of the reasons ice machines have been removed from the sleeping room floors of many hotels. Your facility may still incur liability if minors are served, intoxicated guests are served, or alcoholic beverages are served outside legal hours. There are other forms of liability. For instance, the resulting court case regarding the *Tailhook Scandal*[3] in which a female was groped in the hallway at a military meeting at the Las Vegas Hilton in 1993. It set a precedent that a host and the hotel can no longer claim that they do not know what is going on within the property.

These days CCSMs are seeing fewer hospitality suites with open bars (*unlimited free drinks*). Companies that used to host these types of functions are not willing to be exposed to liabilities anymore.

Vendors Can Be an Upsell

Promoting vendors that enhance a meeting and pay a commission back to the hotel could be considered an upsell. For example, if you are doing an international reception, you could outsource the Japanese booth to a local restaurant, and add a 20-percent commission on top of what the restaurant charges. In this case, the fee would normally be paid by the planner.

Or, if you recommend a florist, the florist can pay a commission directly to the hotel.

In addition to meeting planner planners, you will work closely with external service providers outside the hotel. In the meeting and events world, these providers are typically event production companies, audio-visual suppliers, exhibition or tradeshow companies, security and third-party planners.

---

[3] https://en.wikipedia.org/wiki/Tailhook_scandal

The service providers that your company recommends are most likely on a preferred vendor list and can include the following:

- Audio-visual
- Exhibition, drayage or décor
- Photographers
- Private security
- Entertainers and DJs
- DMCs (*destination management companies*)
- Décorators and florists
- Transportation
- Language translation
- Custom linen
- Car rental
- Printing and business-related services
- Furniture rental
- Wedding planner and suppliers of wedding products and services

When working with outside vendors the planner brings aboard, your relationships with these providers is quite important to the overall success of catering, meeting, and convention events. The most important detail for managing these relationships is to communicate what your meeting planner has sent, e-mailed or shared in a phone conversation with these providers. A CCSM can learn not only to be an extension of the meeting planner's team but also of the service provider's team too. This must be true for both the providers your company recommends, as well as those providers the planners contract on their own with. Many of the planner's preferred providers travel nationally and internationally with them on various events throughout the year. These providers have an advantage over you as they have relationships that have matured year after year, event after event. A CCSM shouldn't compete with this relationship, but rather acknowledge it and deliver the same excellent customer service to them as you would to your main planner. This service will be rewarded with equal respect from both your main planner and your planner's providers. Working with these companies allows the CCSM to learn additional services and styles from those they see on a daily basis with in-house providers.

However, when a planner has not committed or might be on-the-fence with a company outside of the preferred list, it can help if the CCSM lets the planner know the plusses for working with the in-house company. The first thing you can mention is the advantage of having equipment onsite, whereas an outside company must ship-in all their equipment. When planners bring in their own audio-visual providers, the in-house audio-visual team always has to supply them with something, anywhere from VGA[4] cables to extension cords, projector bulbs, laptops, screens, and power-strips. Then there is the insider knowledge that only an in-house provider's technicians know about your specific hotel, including hidden infrastructure, how to connect and disconnect sound in flexible meeting space that has multiple rooms. Most notably, they can communicate with all the hotel staff to get quick answers and fixes that an outside company would *"spin-their-wheels"* and waste precious event setup time trying to learn—things like getting lights turned on and off, and meeting rooms locked for the night. Another consideration is the cost the planner incurs for providing these companies' staff people with lodging, food, and beverage, which can be substantial.

For some facilities, a preferred provider may have to earn a spot on an annual list of providers, while others may be contracted to be on a hotel's preferred list with commission paid back to the hotel or facilities. Often the preferred providers have a vested interest in the property, such as providing tenant improvements to the structure and infrastructure. These providers may rent event space or are given space within the hotel.

Most hotels or facilities allow any planner-chosen service or product provider to work within their building if they are locally or state licensed and insured, including providing a certificate of insurance listing your company as additional insured.

A CCSM will need to inform these providers with written expectations and directions of load-in and out procedures to your building(s) and

---

[4] Video Graphics Array.

any other guidelines your company stipulates. Any and all extra effort and wisdom a CCSM puts forth for the planner with outside companies will help alleviate many unanticipated issues in the mutual goal of achieving excellence in collaboration.

Inside Versus Outside Suppliers

It is important to understand the difference between inside and outside provided services and to be able to analyze the advantages and disadvantages of each. Most events and meetings require more than basic room sets and food and drink. Audio-visual equipment is the most common extra service used. Other services include floral, other décor and props, photography, videography, entertainment, transportation, security, computer rental, printing, furniture, ice carvings, pipe and drape, Wi-Fi, and so on.

For example, most hotels do not want to operate an audio-visual department because the capital outlay is extensive, the equipment needs to be maintained and becomes obsolete quickly, and they would need to hire technicians. But, many hotels and resorts are far from convention cities and may not have audio-visual companies in their area. In this case, they would be forced to buy their own equipment.

Combination of inside and outside services: the facility may have basic equipment, such as microphones. More complex equipment would need to be rented from an audio-visual company. This allows you to negotiate away microphone charges, depending on the value of their business. It is a soft cost.

Many hotels have preferred AV providers that are headquartered with the hotel space with the CCSM team. These companies invest in the hotel's infrastructure to upgrade the lighting, power, rigging points etc. This is invaluable to the hotel and an important topic a CCSM must communicate to planners. Especially those that typically travel with their own preferred AV.

CHAPTER 13

Accounting for Catering and Convention Services

Traditionally, accounting in the hotel business starts with a budget. A budget is a projection of income for a future time period, usually a calendar year. To understand the budgeting process for many catering and convention services (*in full-service hotel properties*), the prerequisite is to understand the hotel business as it relates to sales of group guest rooms.

Once the group room sales goals are established for the future time period (*i.e., next year*), then the amount of food and beverage revenue per room night calculation from catering, meeting, and convention groups can be placed into the budget. Also added into the budget are the contracted group food and beverage minimums for the year's budgeting.

The difference between the group goal and the contracted minimums are usually an educated guess—based in large part upon prior years' historical performance—by the executive team preparing the budget.

Usually these budgets are aggressive, and in fact mandatory in terms of reaching the established goals. The CCSM will therefore search for opportunities to upsell whenever and to whatever extent possible. When they review a file turnover and group history, a CCSM has a good idea of what are appropriate targets for extra revenue.

However, there are some groups where the meeting planner will adamantly announce they will only spend their contracted food and beverage minimum.

And unfortunately, there are planners that know if they don't spend their contracted food and beverage minimum they will be charged the difference without the tax and service fees, which actually is spending less. However, a CCSM must not be overly discouraged, as not all planners disclose their true budgets. Additionally, one small windfall can change these scenarios, such as a sponsor paying for an added tradeshow event, vendors wanting to host an already-scheduled event (*thus giving the planner added funds to spend elsewhere*) or perhaps a newly elected (*at the conference*) board of directors deciding to host a meeting or dinner.

Accounting positions within hotel or facilities can include:

- Night auditors
- Auditors
- Accountants
- Accounting clerks (*accounts payable, accounts receivable*)
- Director of accounting
- Compliance
- Analytics

Those that are unique to casinos hotels include:

- Casino cage staff who count, sort, and record cash and gaming chips for the public behind a protected desk area referred to as *the cage*
- Slot attendants or cashiers on the gaming floor; however, this position is being phased out due to the automation of ticketless gaming

As a CCSM, and depending on your specific hotel's billing requirements, the accounting process can be overwhelming. You may be responsible for collecting all contracted deposits and final pre- and postconference payments. Or you might be required just to inform the accounting team on the current spending for them to bill.

Circumstances that might stand in the way of timely accounting could include your accounting team not being physically at the property where you are located, or that they work within a governmental or quasi-governmental facility that has additional jurisdictions that oversee them.

The primary accounting responsibility of a CCSM is to collect deposits and payments, and to follow up to ensure that planners receive final invoices.

A CCSM may be asked by the director, for projections on a particular group's spending. This information can be used for forecasting purposes.

Periodic forecasts are typically prepared for the upcoming month, 90 days and 6 months. Additionally, they may be asked for input into future capital projects they foresee as needing attention for repairs or replacements.

A CCSM working in a high-volume hotel may be assigned as many as 100 groups a year. Each group will have a contract unique to them, and the billing arrangements may be unique as well. To stay on top of this, your good organizational and recording skills are imperative. Along with these, having a stellar administrative assistant and accounting team are invaluable.

Knowing and communicating to the planner what can be applied to the contract food and beverage minimum is a delicate process. Traditionally, this includes catering food and beverage only. It doesn't include the added tax and service charge, and often a new meeting planner will not understand this; it then falls on the CCSM to clarify this point. A rule of thumb is that whatever is consumed by the guests applies to the food and beverage minimum. However, the exceptions to this can be water stations.

Also, the planner may feel that food purchased in the hotel at restaurant outlets should apply or that guest room service charges should apply and typically this is not the case. However, in some larger properties and in casino environments contracted large-group restaurant events may apply a percentage of revenue toward the convention contracted food and beverage minimum.

However, many hotel restaurants, especially in Las Vegas, are not operated by the hotel. They are leased to restaurant chains or celebrity chefs. What is spent in these independent restaurants will not count toward a planner's F&B *minimum spend*.

Unique to casino properties are gaming regulations; you must learn those that apply to your realm of operations and be able to communicate them to the planner as necessary. An example of this might be when planners want to purchase gaming chips for giveaways at tradeshows, incentive events, and raffles; this is illegal and planners must be advised of this.

Depending on the employer and the size of their property, CCSMs may have to know the intricacies of what are taxable and nontaxable revenue sources. For example, room rental may be nontaxable but charging chef labor fees may be taxable. Additionally, some state laws require that service charges added to the menu price for catered events be taxed. Sometimes this tax process is complex to figure out if the law states the service charge only relating to the amount of gratuity is not taxed but the amount of the service charge that is profit for the house is taxed.

Other accounting processes can involve consideration of:

- LET (*live entertainment tax*) which is collected when live entertainment is offered and the group is charging a per person ticket price for the event versus the event being included in the overall convention registration fee
- In-house events that are not taxed and contracted union labor is charged
- In-house events that are complimentary for some guests while other guests pay a per-ticket charge gets multifaceted in the accounting, for both tax and reporting purposes
- Public cash food and bar offerings that have their own nuances in accounting and recording

Among the forms and documents used by CCSMs for planners and their affiliates are:

- Credit card authorization forms and the process to charge completed forms
- Direct billing applications and the approval process
- Invoices for deposits and final payments
- Banquet event order checks—listing the total individual event cost with tax and service charge
- Paid out cash forms
- Guestroom portfolios (*folios*)

In addition, the CCSM will use internal forms and develop a knowledge of:

- Miscellaneous auditing and tracing forms specific for your company
- Employee incentive tracking forms
- Budget spreadsheets
- Profit and loss statements (*P&Ls*)

Final accounting is frequently the one of the least favorite duties of a CCSM. Once a group is completed—meaning that all the contracted events and concessions are done and the guests have all checked out—the CCSM has moved on to the next group. But they can be forced to go back and resurrect their thinking about the previous group when accounting stumbling blocks arise; these can include discrepancies on the final bill, disputed charges on consumption and room charges to the master account, and so on. Often the CCSM has long forgotten the details and needs to review correspondence of old e-mails, tons of filed paperwork including the contract, BEOs, banquet checks, and draw upon memory recall of conversations with planners from months earlier.

Control Procedures

Control procedures must be used to ensure that actual performance is in line with planned performance. When a planner purchases a catered event, they are buying something that doesn't yet exist.

The control cycle begins when a planner considers booking business at a property and it does not end until the catered function is completed to everyone's satisfaction. Before a control system can be implemented, there must be set standards of performance.

If you book a beverage function and expect each bottle of liquor to yield approximately 15 drinks, the actual number of drinks served per container must be consistent with this standard.

If bartenders pour more or less than 15 drinks per container, there may be a control problem. If they pour too many drinks per container, usually the guests are receiving a reduced portion size. If they pour too few drinks per container, chances are there is excessive waste or guests are receiving excessive portion sizes.

Standard Operating Procedures

It's hotel management's duty to set required standards and policies by which all catered events will be run.

All operational procedures, from booking the business, to purchasing, receiving, storing, issuing, producing, and serving the finished products, to function-room selection and setup, to final bill tabulation and collection, must be standardized.

If hotel employees follow standard operating procedures (SOPs), chances are you will reach your cost-control and quality control goals with minimal difficulty.

Credit Management

If a planner is eligible for credit, the hotel's credit manager will evaluate the planner's credit rating and, if credit is approved, set up a master account number. He or she will then detail the property's deposit requirements and billing procedures.

Generous credit terms can be a marketing advantage for a hotel. A planner may select a property because it offers generous credit terms.

Breakeven Analysis

Many people backed into this industry and never studied any basic business concepts. So, here is a quick and dirty look at what breakeven analysis is and how to use it.

The breakeven point is where revenues are equal to expenses.

First, you have to understand the difference between *fixed costs* and *variable costs*.

Fixed costs are costs that do not change, regardless of the number of guests. They include speaker fees, room rental, audio-visual, utilities, staff salaries, and so on.

Variable costs are tied to the number of guests. You only guarantee food and beverage based on the number of guests, you only order the number of shuttle busses based on attendance, and so on.

Total costs are a combination of fixed and variable costs (FC + VC = TC)

Consider the registration fee. To calculate how many guests a planner will need to cover all of the expenses (*the breakeven point*), subtract the variable costs from the registration fee to get the *contribution margin*. Then, divide the total fixed cost by the contribution margin.

For example:

- If the registration fee is $300 and the fixed costs are $5,000 for the meeting room rental, $1,000 for audio-visual, and $4,000 for a speaker = $10,000 in fixed costs.
- And if the variable costs are $200 per person, subtract the $200 variable cost from the $300 registration fee, which leaves $100.
- Divide the $100 contribution margin into the $10,000 total fixed cost and you see that the planner will need 100 guests to break even.

Once the planner's breakeven point has been reached and their fixed costs are covered, they only have to pay the variable costs on additional guests. So, if out of the $300 registration fee before breakeven, $100 goes to for fixed costs and $200 to variable costs, after the breakeven point the planner is only paying the $200 in variable costs and that $100 goes directly to the bottom line of a planner's budget.

You don't even have to do the math. There are a number of online Breakeven Analysis Calculators, such as this one that even creates a graph. http://fast4cast.com/break-even-calculator.aspx

The sample graph shows the Breakeven Point (BEP), Variable Costs (VC), Fixed Costs (FC), and Profit or Contribution Margin (CM). You can see that once you make your BEP, your only costs are the variable costs, so profit increases the number of attendees (Figure 13.1).

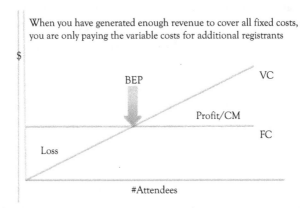

Figure 13.1 Breakeven Point

If a CCSM knows these costs or can estimate (*based on reading online registration fees*), they will know how to recommend other goods and services as well increase as food and beverage revenues.

Business Letter Writing

While there are many types of formats, the easiest to learn is called the Block Style, which does not indent or center. Everything is left justified (*with a one inch margin*). It is simple, quick, and easy.

If you are writing on behalf of your company and using letterhead (*imprinted stationary*), you would leave out the address block on the example below. And, be sure you type your title under your name. If possible, keep the letter to one page. If more pages are needed, be sure to number them 1 of 3 or 2 of 5. If it is a letter of agreement, which can serve as a contract, be sure each page is dated and initialed with a place for a return signature on the last page.

If you are writing a personal cover letter to accompany a resume, follow the example.

Leave a double space between every element of the letter, except leave four spaces for your signature. Paragraphs should be single space, with double space between them.

You should always state why you are writing in the first paragraph. People are busy and mostly scan written documents today. Don't make them read to the end to see what you are asking or telling them. The first paragraph should not be longer than four lines. Only one topic per paragraph—don't muddy the waters. Break up big blocks of text.

Never start with I, me, or we. Bring the reader into the letter first. This is called the *"you attitude."*

A colon should be used after the salutation, not a comma.

The best font size is 12. The best font is a sans serif type, meaning clean lines (*such as Arial, Verdana, or Calibri*), not one with curly cues. Never, ever use Comic Sans.

Don't use all caps. It is considered to be shouting.

Typical closings seem archaic. Who actually says Sincerely, Respectfully Yours or Yours Truly out loud? *"Cordially"* is preferable for most letters. It is friendly. If you know the person well enough, you can use *"Warmly."* A comma goes after the closing.

If you are including enclosures, after your signature, add: Enc.1 or Enc.2, depending on how many enclosures you have. This will alert the reader that something is missing if the noted number of items are not enclosed.

Sample Block Style Letter
1234 Easy Street
Las Vegas NV 89109

October 11, 2018

Dear Mr. Smith:

Thank you for meeting with me on Monday regarding the sales position available at your Atlanta hotel. I greatly appreciate the time you spent reviewing my career goals and recommending strategies for achieving them. Your advice was very helpful and I now have a new perspective on available opportunities.

I especially appreciate your offer to connect me to others in your network. I plan on following up with the contacts you e-mailed me right away. I will also use the online networking resources you recommended to further my job search.

Any additional suggestions you may have would be welcome. I'll update you as my search progresses.

Again, thank you so much for your help. I greatly appreciate the assistance you have provided me. I am enclosing an updated resume.

Cordially,

Mary Jones
Enc. 1

Wrapping Up Your Events with a Pretty Bow

Just before the end of a multiday conference, ask your planner if they would like to schedule a postconvention meeting or conference call. Prior to that be sure to have checked on their contentment level each day of their events.

If time permits send the planner or planners a final-night amenity. Be sure the amenity is either small or easy to consume, like chocolate-covered strawberries and small bottles of water, or something light weight they can take home to their family like prepackaged macaroons (*avoid items like bottles of wine*) or offer to take them out to happy hour or dinner.

Also, inform the planner on the final billing process and when they can expect receive the final invoice and from whom.

From the beginning, typically at the preconvention meeting, you have asked for the planner to fill out the event-satisfaction survey upon completion of the events. Give a final reminder and instructions on how to complete the survey and when it is due, if necessary. Keep in mind your planner or planners have been so busy for months getting ready for their events, have often times traveled long distances and spent several days away from their home and families to work the events with long days and nights. The last thing on their mind is your survey completion. However, it is foremost on your mind, especially if you are rated on getting the return survey or are personally incentivized on achieving the highest score on the survey.

Additionally, if you have associate reward programs, please advise the planner before, during, and at the end of their events. These planner-nominated rewards are very important to associate morale and confidence, as well as being kept in their employee files for future reviews and promotion considerations. Please reward all frontline and hourly associates with client comments of going above and beyond with their service. If the planner doesn't have time to complete these recognition forms, offer to do it on their behalf. Also advise them of any back-of-the-house associates they perhaps didn't get a chance to meet but were essential to the success of their events. This could be the administrative assistant in the setup department that coordinated their unexpected and last-minute room setup changes, the cook in the pastry shop that whipped up a same-day cake for the planner's CEO's wife's birthday, or the concierge that found the closest costume shop for the 80s wig the planner needed for the general session that begins in just a few hours.

Finally, at the conclusion of each event—whether a small meeting, a destination wedding, or large convention group—a simple thank you for the opportunity to be of service is always appropriate. Take the time to handwrite this thank you or send an e-mail from the heart. Welcome them back to your property and let them know the business, partnership and, most importantly, their friendship was appreciated!

Glossary

Every industry has its jargon, and catering is no different. Here are some terms you should know:

A la Carte: each menu item is priced individually as opposed to an entire menu for one fixed price.

A la Minute: food that is prepared to order, not preassembled or precooked and held in hot boxes. An option in some hotels for small VIP groups.

Amuse Bouche: a single small bite size piece of food served prior to the meal.

APEX: an initiative of the Convention Industry Council (CIC) to standardize industry paperwork.

App: a computerized application downloadable to a mobile device.

Attrition: financial penalties for not meeting a guarantee, room block, and so on.

Auditorium or Theater Set: rows of chairs, no tables.

Banquet Event Order (BEO)*:* a document signed by planners that shows agreed items food, beverage, chef and stewarding notes, schedule of events, meetings and tradeshow, room setup, audio-visual information or contact, billing, and master accounts.

Breakout Room: smaller meeting room used for breakout sessions.

Breakout Session: concurrent session—sessions that are occurring simultaneously.

C-Level: upper level management such as CEO, COO, CFO, and so on.

Change Log: used to communicate a change to the BEO in the CRM system that is distributed to all operations departments.

Change Order: a form used to by banquet servers onsite to inform essential parties of any changes to the BEO.

Chef Tourant: a chef that works all stations, filling in on other chef's days off.

Cherrypicker: a hydraulic crane with a raised platform used to raise and lower people.

Citywide Conventions: conventions that use all or most of the hotels in a destination.

Classroom Set: chairs with tables in front of them.

Corkage: a fee charged per bottle for opening and serving wine brought in by the planner or a sponsor.

Cover: this term actually has three meanings. One, it is the cloche or lid that keeps the food warm. Two, it is the place setting on the table (*flatware, glasses, napkin, etc.*). Three, it is the number of people served. "*We had 500 covers tonight.*"

CRM: Customer Relationship Management.

CSM: Catering Service Manager or Convention Service Manager.

CCSM: Catering and Convention Services Manager (*combined at uniserve hotels*).

Consideration: payment in money, product or services.

Continental Breakfast: coffee and tea, juice, and some type of bread (*bagel, muffin, Danish, etc.*).

Contract Concessions: items in a sales contract that are uniquely offered.

Cumulative Basis: the total sum for the entire event dates.

Drill-Down: an industry term meaning to "*fact find*" by asking all questions until the answers reveal facts and expectations.

Dualing or Duet Menus: this is another term for Split Entrees. Instead of having an 8-ounce steak, you can have a 4-ounce steak and a 4-ounce piece of fish (*surf and turf*). This is a good way to introduce exotic items to a meat and potato crowd. It also allows guests to "*trade*" an item they do not like.

Entourage: a group of people surrounding an important person, including bodyguards, family, managers, agents, public relations people, friends, hair stylist, makeup artist, and so on.

Executive Pastry Chef: in-charge of baking breads and creating desserts.

Executive Steward: oversees staff responsible for the cleanliness of the kitchen area, including sanitation, dishwashing, and so on. Manages the inventory. Requisition forms are sent to the stewarding office to request the number of plates, knives, forks, glasses, and so on, be delivered to a function room.

Family Style Service: platter set on table and passed around by guests.

FF&E or FFE: Furniture, Fixtures, and Equipment. A budgeting category that hotels and facilities will use to allocate funds for the replacement or remodeling of soft goods, which are items not attached to the structure of a building. In the catering conventions service world this relates to banquet equipment and china, glass, and silverware items.

Ganging Menus or Menu Match: this is when two or more groups in-house serve the same menu. Chefs love this, because they can get quantity discounts when purchasing larger quantities of specific items, such as filet mignon. It is also easier in the kitchen and often requires less labor to have everyone working on the same menu.

Garde Manger: a chef that makes cold salads, sandwiches, appetizers, and desserts.

General Session: plenary session, a session designed for all guests.

GRA: Guest Room Attendants. Housekeeping department staff that are responsible for cleaning hotel guestrooms.

Group Resume: a packet containing all information about a group and their activities. Includes all BEOs, setup instructions, décor, and other requirements.

Guarantee: the planner guarantees the number of guests that will be attending an event and must pay for that number even if they don't all show up.

Hospitality Desk: offering drinks, snacks, and information during check-in.

In-house: groups that are already checked into the hotel and have begun events.

In-house Meetings: internal meetings for the hotel staff and paid for by the hotel.

Intermezzo: an intermission in meal service just before the main course. Sorbet is usually served, to cleanse the palate.

Internal Planner: associates within the planner's or hotel's organization.

Lectern: a table or floor stand with a sloping top to hold a book or notes, and from which someone, a speaker can read while standing up. Often called a podium.

LET: Live Entertainment Tax.

LGBTQ: Lesbian, Gay, Bisexual, Transgender, Questioning.

Market Price or AQ (As Quoted): used in place of a set price on a menu item where the price shifts seasonally or where prices fluctuate greatly.

Napery: tablecloths, overlays, runners, napkins, and other linens used on the dining table.

Nonprofit Events: typically charity fundraisers.

"on the floor": working in the convention or conference center area.

Pit Boss: an employee in a casino in charge of gaming tables.

Plenary Session: general session with programming for all guests.

Podium: see Lectern.

Post-Con: a meeting held immediately following the end of an event for the purpose of evaluating and reviewing what happened at the event.

Pre-Con: a meeting held immediately prior to the start of an event for the purpose of reviewing all elements of the event. Attended by management from the hotel and the meeting planners.

Resort Fees: a mandatory daily additional charge separated out from the advertised guest room price by a hotel.

Resume: a document containing the contracted group confirmed plans. Resumes are used as the main communication tool to hotel operation departments and are typically e-mailed, reviewed at resume meeting, and presented at the pre-con. This multipage document includes: group profile, rooms pick up to contract, VIP arrangements, transportation, notes to various hotel departments, and so on.

Rigger: specializes in lifting and moving large or heavy objects, often with a crane or *cherry-picker*, used to hang trusses and ceiling treatments.

Room Amenities: food, beverage or gift items sent to a guest room typically through room service.

Room Drops: similar to room amenities, but can include sponsored marketing materials and planner information. This can include group bag pull and departure notices.

Rider: a document outlining what an entertainer(s) requirements are for a contracted service. An amendment to an entertainment contract.

Silencer: padding under the tablecloth used to quiet the clatter of dishes, cups, and flatware. A *"must"* when having speakers during a meal.

Site Visit or Inspection: a planner makes a visit to the hotel to see if it is appropriate for their event. The planner checks things like amount of square feet available, parking, food and beverage options, accessibility, and so on.

SMERF: Social, Military, Education, Religious, and Fraternal. Low-budget business groups.

Staffing Guide: a scheduling and control tool used to determine the number of labor hours, number of staff needed, and the estimated labor cost needed to service an event.

Swags: swaths of cloth, typically hung from the ceiling.

Tasting: a meeting with prospective planners where potential menu items are sampled.

Third-Party Planners: a professional meeting planning company hired to provide services such as hotel site locations, reservation coordination, onsite conference coordination, and so on.

Uniserve Hotel: a hotel where catering and convention services are combined and one CCSM handles all aspects of the event.

Upgrade: to raise something to a higher standard, typically by improving, adding or replacing components.

Upsell: a sales technique where a seller convinces the buyer to purchase more expensive items, upgrades or other add-ons to increase revenue, and create a more memorable event.

Waived Charges: no extra charge for a third and fourth guest in a guestroom.

Whales: high rollers, those that gamble highly in casinos.

For more industry terminology, consult the APEX Glossary from the Convention Industry Council (CIC): http://www conventionindustry org/ APEX/glossary aspx.

Appendix

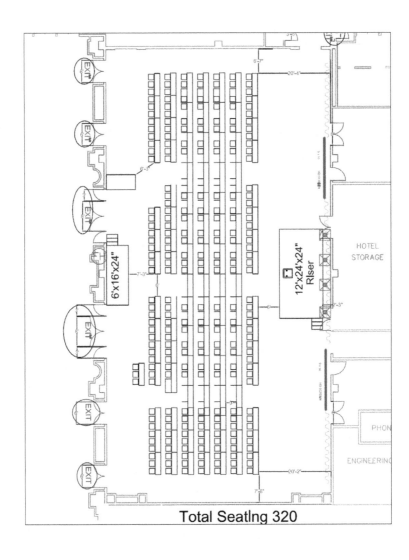

Total Seating 320

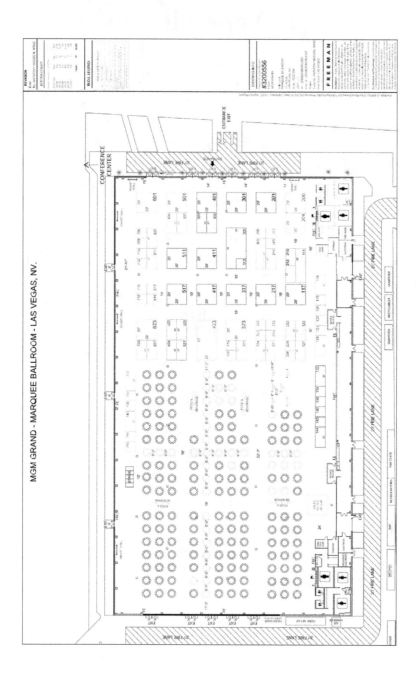

MGM GRAND - MARQUEE BALLROOM - LAS VEGAS, NV.

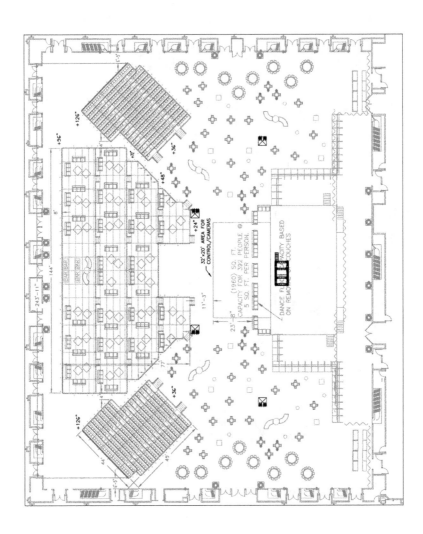

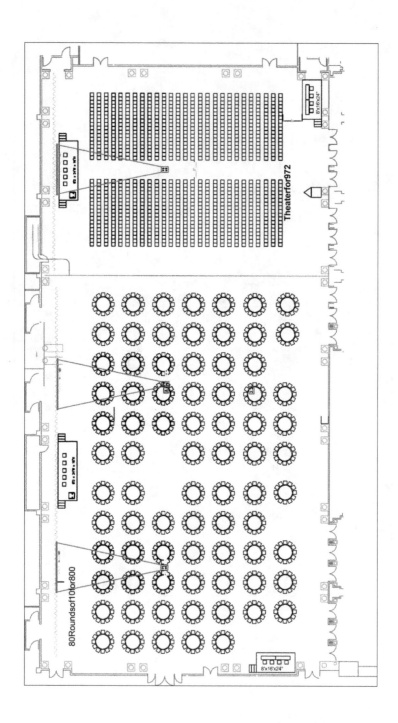

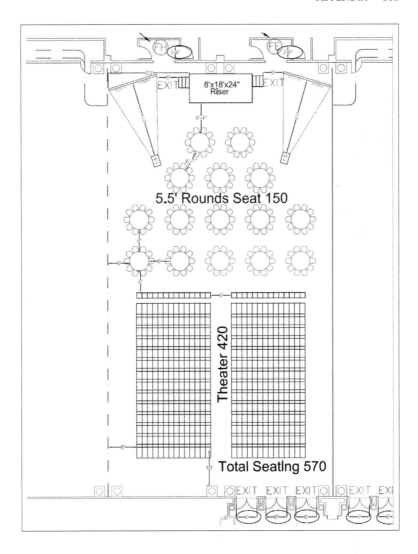

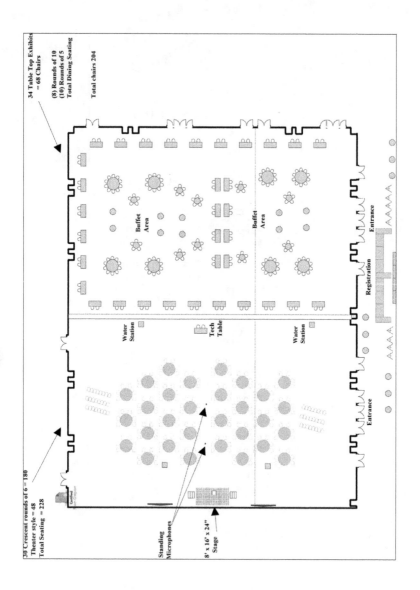

Index